Mastering Proje‹

Key skills

aⁱiᵘ successful projects

Mastering Project Management

Key skills in ensuring profitable and successful projects

Cathy Lake

THORO**g**OOD

Published by

Thorogood Ltd

12-18 Grosvenor Gardens

London SW1W 0DH

0171 824 8257

A catalogue record for this book is available from the British Library

ISBN 1-85418-062-2

Printed in Great Britain by Ashford Colour Press

The author

Cathy Lake MA(Oxon)

After leaving Oxford University with a degree in English, Cathy Lake worked for the educational publishers Thomas Nelson & Sons Ltd. Since 1976, she has worked as a freelance editor, writer and project manager. During the past two decades, she has taken part in, and also managed, almost every aspect of the publishing process. She has worked for most of the major national publishers and has written about 40 training manuals and textbooks, mainly on management and health-related topics. She recently contributed six workbooks to the Institute of Management Open Learning Programme.

Cathy has worked as a project manager on several large publishing projects and is currently involved with the development of multimedia learning materials. She lives in Cornwall with her husband and two children.

Contents

Icons

Throughout the Masters in Management series of books you will see references and symbols in the margins. These are designed for ease of use and quick reference directing you quickly to key features of the text. The symbols used are:

 Key Question

 Action Checklist   Key Learning Point

 Activity   Key Management Concept

We would encourage you to use this book as a workbook, writing notes and comments in the margin as they occur. In this way we hope that you will benefit from the practical guidance and advice which this book provides.

Introducing
project management

Chapter 1

Project management is not the same as ordinary, day-to-day operational management. When you are managing the ongoing operations of an organisation, your main concerns are stability and continuity. You try to set up systems which will produce the desired results day in, day out, month after month, perhaps even year after year. When these systems are in place, you must constantly look for ways in which they can be refined and improved to make them more efficient and effective, but you are, in essence, dealing with a permanent situation which will probably outlast your own involvement with it.

Project management is different. Here, your aim is to achieve a limited set of objectives within an agreed amount of time and an agreed budget. As a project manager, you will probably see the project through from start to finish – and the ultimate success or failure of the scheme will have a lot to do with the decisions you take along the way. You make the plans and you monitor the way they are carried out.

In operational management, there are established lines of communication and command, leading from the factory floor (or its equivalent) to the Managing Director. If you need advice or something goes wrong, you know where you can turn to within the organisation. In a project, everything focuses on the project manager. You are at the centre of a team of people with differing skills who may well be working together for the first time. It is your task to focus their talents and energy on the objectives you want to achieve.

Project management demands highly developed planning skills, leadership qualities, an understanding of the priorities and concerns of your team, a sensitivity to the culture of the environment in which you are working, the ability to know when to take a calculated risk – and a greatly increased level of personal commitment. Project management is not an easy ride. But it offers opportunities and responsibilities which are only usually available in operational management to those people who reach a very senior level.

In this first chapter we will examine the defining characteristics of project management. We will also discuss some of the issues – such as the role of stakeholders, what happens at the various stages of a project and the importance of balancing time, money and quality – which preoccupy project managers. By the end of the chapter you should have a built a firm foundation to which you can add the practical techniques discussed in later chapters.

What exactly is a project?

Three project managers met at a training course. In the first session, they introduced themselves and described the projects on which they were currently working:

- *'I'm in charge of the construction of a retail development in the centre of a large town. There are 26 retail units and a supermarket in the complex. My main responsibilities are to co-ordinate the work of the various contractors to ensure that the project is completed to specification, within budget and on time.'*

- *'I am directing a team of research scientists. We are running trials on a new analgesic drug on behalf of a pharmaceutical company. It is my responsibility to design the experiments and make sure that proper scientific and legal procedures are followed, so that our results can be subjected to independent statistical analysis.'*

- *'The international aid agency which employs me is sending me to Central America to organise the introduction of multimedia resources at a teachers' training college. My role is quite complex. I have to make sure that appropriate resources are purchased – and in some cases developed within the college. I also have to encourage the acceptance of these resources by lecturers and students within the college.'*

On the face of it, these three projects appear to have little in common. They have been set up to achieve very different outcomes: a shopping complex, a new drug and a new method of teaching students. Clearly, a project is not defined by the type of outcome it is set up to achieve. It is not, as they say, *what* you do, but the *way* that you do it.

Projects can be set up for a wide variety of purposes. They exist in all sectors of industry and in every type of organisation. Some projects are also much more complicated than others. The Association for Project Management recognises four levels of projects:

- An in-house project involving a single disciplinary team

- An in-house project involving a multidisciplinary team

- A multicompany multidisciplinary project

- A multicountry multicompany multidisciplinary project.

Project management skills are needed at each of these levels, but the challenges increase as projects become more complex. In a single disciplinary in-house project, the people involved have probably worked together before. They understand each others' functions and are familiar with how things are done within the organisation. At the other end of the scale, the project manager may have to co-ordinate the efforts of people who:

- Are geographically distant

- Do not speak the same language

- Are working within different cultural and legal frameworks

- Are working for different organisations

- Do not understand each others' roles.

However, all projects, whatever their scale and proposed outcome, share certain basic characteristics.

Key Management Concept

A project is a temporary endeavour involving a connected sequence of activities and a range of resources, which is designed to achieve a specific and unique outcome and which operates within time, cost and quality constraints and which is often used to introduce change.

This is a complex definition. We need to look at its separate elements in more detail.

Projects are temporary. They have a limited life. Unlike the ongoing operations of organisations, projects cease when the results they were set up to achieve have been accomplished. (However, the shopping complex, drug or teaching method will continue in existence, perhaps for many years, after the project which brought it into being has ended.)

Projects are established to achieve specific outcomes. In a 'hard project', the outcome is something which has a physical reality, such as a building, a bridge or a new product. A 'soft project', on the other hand, is designed to achieve a less tangible kind of result, such as a new process or an organisational change. In either case, the outcomes are decided at the beginning, at the very start of the project.

Because projects invariably result in something new, they always bring about change of some kind. The change may be relatively unimportant, and be easily assimilated by the people it affects. Or it may have very significant consequences. A project manager therefore needs to be aware of management techniques which can be used to overcome resistance to change.

Every project is unique. If you have built an office building in one location and are then asked to build an identical building on another site, you will find that you are faced with a new set of challenges. The geology may be slightly different. The weather conditions may not be the same. You will probably be working with a different team, with different skills and personalities. The uniqueness of projects calls for a distinctive approach to management. Instead of trying to maintain an established and stable process, you must constantly think of new solutions to new problems.

Projects have time, cost and quality constraints. The triangle of time, cost and quality lies at the heart of project management. It is the project manager's task to achieve the required outcomes within a pre-determined schedule and budget, whilst maintaining quality standards. When a project is being planned, and also while it is underway, it is necessary to balance these three interrelated elements.

The outcome of a project can only be achieved by the completion of a variety of separate, but linked, activities. In a small project, these activities may be performed by the same multi-skilled individual or individuals. More usually, they require a team of people who have different types of technical skill or specialist knowledge. Most of the tools and techniques which are associated with project management are used as aids to plan and monitor this sequence of activities.

As a project progresses, different types of resources are required. Among other things, these resources may include: people with specific skills, equipment, raw materials, premises, information and transport. Without these inputs, the activities which make up a project cannot proceed. It is one of the chief responsibilities of the project manager to ensure that the necessary resources are available when they are required.

Projects need leadership. Projects involve the co-ordination of different resources to achieve a predetermined result. One person, the project manager, needs to maintain an overall vision of the goal and a detailed understanding of the progress that has been made towards this goal. Project teams are usually made up of people with complementary, and consequently different, areas of expertise. It is up to the project manager to co-ordinate – and provide direction to – their efforts.

What is project management?

Projects are not a modern phenomenon. Think, for example, of the pyramids of Egypt, the Great Wall of China or the Aztec temples. In actual fact, the results of major building projects are all that remain of many ancient civilisations. These edifices could only have been constructed by organising the efforts and skills of a large number of people. They were clearly built to a specific plan and changed the physical, and perhaps the cultural, environment. They have most of the characteristics of the projects we recognise today. However, they were not built using the techniques of project management.

Project management has a much shorter history. Its origins lie in World War II, when the military authorities used the techniques of operational research to plan the optimum use of resources. One of these techniques was the use of networks to represent a system of related activities. In 1961 the US Navy published details of a planning technique which had been developed on the Polaris programme. They claimed that they had saved two years' time by using this method, which was called 'Programme Evaluation and Review Technique', or PERT. At about the same time, a similar technique, known as the 'Critical Path Method' was described by Du Pont, a large US chemical corporation. Both these techniques used network diagrams to plan the most effective way to use resources in complex projects. These techniques were quickly adopted for use in many different contexts and are now indispensable tools of the trade for project managers.

It was the need to achieve results quickly which precipitated the development of the modern techniques of project management. In Ancient Egypt, it was possible to take a generation to build the Great Pyramid. Nowadays, things have to happen a great deal more rapidly. In war and in business, it is essential to be ahead of the opposition. Time also has a money value. When funds are invested in a commercial project, they have to produce a return which is better than (or at least equal to) that which could be achieved on the open market. The longer it takes to complete a commercial project, the higher the returns that are expected from it.

Key Management Concept

Defining project management

Here is a classic definition of project management:

'The application of a collection of tools and techniques to direct the use of diverse resources toward the accomplishment of a unique, complex, one time task within time, cost and quality constraints'. (1)

We will explore this 'collection of tools and techniques' later in the book. As well as network diagrams and the critical path method (which is more commonly known as critical path management or critical path analysis) they include Gantt charts and the work breakdown structure. The project manager uses these tools to:

- Organise the component tasks in the most logical order

- Plan the optimum use of resources

- Build schedules and other documents to monitor the progress of the project.

Most of these tools and techniques are available in the form of computer software and it is quite possible for anyone to use these programs with the minimum of training. Some people assume that mastery of these tools of the trade will turn them into instant project managers. However, these same people would probably not be very confident about consulting a doctor who had simply learnt how to write out a prescription form. Although you can go out and buy a box of software with 'Project Management' on the lid, you cannot learn the skills of project management quite so easily. The science, and the art, of the profession lies in knowing when and how to use the tools in a real, and rapidly changing, situation.

The body of knowledge

In recent years, there have been several attempts to describe and classify what project managers need to know. Various versions of this body of knowledge have been developed by organisations around the world. The following framework has been developed by the Association of Project Managers in the UK (2). These are the areas in which a Certificated Project Manager needs to have knowledge and experience:

Project management
This relates to the structure and organisation of projects and programmes. It includes an understanding of the project life cycle and of systems management.

Project environment
This area of knowledge is concerned with the interface between the project and the organisation on whose behalf it is set up. It includes project strategy and appraisal, integration, close-out and post-project appraisal.

Organisation and people
This area is concerned with methods of organisation design, control and co-ordination. It also includes the skills needed to lead and communicate with the project team.

Processes and procedures
This covers planning and control, including scheduling, performance measurement, value management and change control.

General management
These are the areas of general management knowledge, such as finance, law, information technology, quality and safety, which may be required in the context of a project just as much as in an operational situation.

Some of these areas of knowledge in this list are specific to project management. Others, such as those involved in 'Organisation and people' and 'General management', are also relevant to managers who are working in non-project environments.

A different list of topics has been developed in the US by the Project Management Institute. In 1987, the PMI published a *Project Management Body of Knowledge* (PMBOK) document which defined the PMBOK as 'all those topics, subject areas and intellectual processes which are involved in the application of sound management principles to... projects.' In 1996, the PMI replaced this with a new publication, *A guide to the project management body of knowledge*. While the PMI acknowledged that it was impossible to contain the entire PMBOK in a single document, it gave the following topics as those which were generally accepted to be necessary to the project manager:

- Project integration management

- Project scope management

- Project time management

- Project cost management

- Project quality management

- Project human resource management

- Project communications management

- Project risk management

- Project procurement management.

Although the way they are organised is different, these two versions of the body of knowledge cover much the same ground.

The project manager

A study (3) of 41 projects in the US asked project managers to describe the tasks that they performed as part of their jobs. The projects were based in five different industries: construction, utilities, pharmaceuticals, information systems and manufacturing. It emerged that 80 per cent of the tasks were the same, suggesting that a large proportion of the skills required by project managers are generic and not specific to the particular industry in which they are working.

Essentially, a project manager has to fulfil four roles. He or she has to be:

- A planner

- A controller

- A leader

- A communicator.

We will examine these four aspects of the job and identify the personal and professional skills they demand.

The project manager as planner

A project is made up of a unique combination of activities, all of which require resources of one kind or another. Each activity will take a certain amount of time to complete and many of them will be dependent on the start or finish of other activities. The project manager has to produce plans which will enable all the necessary activities to take place in the appropriate order, at the right cost and to an acceptable standard.

The first plans for a project are made on a broad, strategic level. Even if the project manager is not personally involved in drawing up these strategic plans, he or she needs to be able to understand the big issues which are at stake. Later in the process, the project manager will certainly have an important role in constructing the detailed project plans. This demands an understanding of planning tools, such as risk assessment techniques and network diagrams. It also requires some degree of familiarity with the type of work involved in the project. The project manager does not need to be an expert in the field, but must know enough to be able to communicate with people who are.

The drawing up of schedules, bills of materials, budgets and other planning documents requires careful attention to detail. As a project manager, you need the ability to switch between a macro and micro view of activities. You must be able to focus down on small, significant details, while retaining an understanding of how they fit into the big picture.

It is also important, at the planning stage of a project, to be sensitive to the organisation which is most closely involved with it. You must understand the structure of this organisation, and be aware of who takes which kind of decision. It is also essential that plans are consistent with the culture of the organisation.

'When I was asked to prepare a promotional video on behalf of a professional association, I decided to involve two people who work in the association's research department. They had in-depth knowledge of the industry and I thought they would welcome the opportunity to provide some input. However, I had not appreciated the fiercely hierarchical structure which operated within the association. The Head of Research was extremely unhappy about two of her staff 'freelancing' on the video. She made things very difficult for them and, in the end, I had to use outside consultants instead.'

Another skill which the project manager needs is the ability to evaluate people. What quality of output will a particular individual be capable of? How quickly will he or she work? Are there likely to be any personality clashes between members of the project team?

Planning a project requires:

- *Knowledge of project management techniques*

- *Some specialist knowledge of the area of work*

- *The ability to take an overview*

- *Attention to detail*

- *An understanding of organisational structure and culture*

- *People skills.*

Action Checklist

The project manager as controller

When a project is underway, progress must be monitored and compared to the plans. There are three crucial questions which the project manager should be able to answer at all times:

- How much have we spent?

- How much have we done?

- How well have we done it?

In order to answer these questions, the project manager needs to track:

- Expenditure against the budget

- Completion of individual tasks against the schedule

- Quality against the pre-determined specifications.

On a project of any size, specialised software is often used to track and report on progress. A project manager clearly needs to be able to use this software competently. When a project is underway, large amounts of information arrive on the project manager's desk. You will need good organisational and data-handling skills to deal promptly and efficiently with this tide of information. If you lack these skills, you may find that you are missing significant facts or that you are actually holding up the progress of the project by monitoring what is going on.

You also need some specialist knowledge of the area of work if you are to oversee progress. This will enable you to decide which aspects of activities need to be checked – and whether the work that has been done is of an acceptable standard. It is unusual for a project manager to be an expert in all the tasks that make up a project. You will almost certainly have to rely on the expertise of other people in some areas. You should, however, be aware of the areas where you need to obtain specialist advice.

'I was organising a conference at which I planned to set up a live video link with a group of academics in the US. I am not an expert in telecommunications, so I employed somebody who was. I asked him to draw up a list of technical specifications and to check that the equipment we hired for the occasion would do the job.'

In any project, things are unlikely to go exactly to plan. You will need to revise and update your schedules and budgets as the work progresses. To do this, you have to achieve a balance between maintaining a strategic overview and paying careful attention to detail. You also need to be flexible at times, and have the ability to find creative solutions to problems.

Action Checklist

Controlling a project requires:

- *Knowledge of project management techniques*
- *Some specialist knowledge of the area of work*
- *Organisational and data-handling skills*
- *The ability to take an overview*
- *Attention to detail*
- *Flexibility*
- *The ability to find creative solutions to problems.*

The project manager as leader

There are several different types of leadership style. As a manager, you may naturally prefer to behave as:

- A facilitator

- An autocrat

- A democrat

- A coach

- A pacesetter

- A path-finder

- An arbitrator

- A spokesperson

As a project manager, you will probably have to vary your style, taking on different roles as the situation demands it. Sometimes you will have to work alongside your team, providing them with the resources and motivation they need to achieve their objectives. At other times you may have to put the interests of the project before the immediate concerns of the team. You may be called upon to mediate between team members who are at loggerheads with each other. You may have to fight to secure the resources which your team needs. At times you may want to concede to the superior specialist knowledge of members of your team, while at other times, you may have to impose an unpopular decision.

Leading a project requires:

- *The ability to adopt a range of leadership styles*

- *The ability to pick the most appropriate style of leadership in any situation.*

Which style of leader are you? Which styles of leadership do you need to learn?

Action Checklist

Key Question

The project manager as communicator

A project manager has to communicate with:

- The project team

- The client

- The outside world, including the press

- Anybody else who is affected by the project.

Some forms of communication, such as reports, press releases, presentations and proposals, have their own conventions and rules, with which you must make yourself familiar. You will also have to devise your own format for other types of communication, such as briefing notes and progress reports. Many of these topics are covered at appropriate points, later in this book.

When you make any type of communication, it is useful to remember these questions:

- What do I want to happen as a result of this communication?

- Who am I communicating with?

- What is the most effective method of communication in this situation?

- How must I adapt my communication to the needs of my audience?

- How am I going to know that my message has been received and understood?

This five-step approach to communication is discussed in more detail in Chapter 4, where we examine the way the project manager communicates with the project team.

Action Checklist

Communicating on a project requires:

- *Competence in a range of communication styles*

- *An understanding of the basic principles of communication*

- *The ability to vary the method, style and content of your communication to the needs of your audience.*

Stages of a project

Projects are divided into several distinct stages. Together, these phases make up the project life cycle. The number of stages, exactly what happens in each of them, and the terminology used to describe them, will differ from project to project, but they usually follow this general pattern:

- Start-up

- Planning and organisation

- Implementation

- Conclusion.

These four phases correspond to the stages in the design cycle:

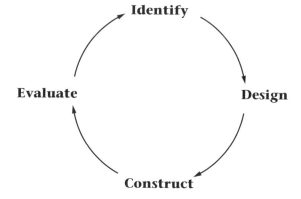

Start-up

This is the stage at which the idea for a project emerges and is given consideration. At this point, there may be several projects in competition for the same funding, and many of them will not be taken any further. Projects which survive to the next stage in the life cycle are those which:

- Are designed to do something worthwhile, AND

- Appear to be capable of achieving their goals.

At the start-up stage, investors look for projects which will meet their needs. The need can take innumerable forms. It could be a reliable return on their cash, a method of entering a new market or reducing costs, a social or organisational problem, a medical condition, a way of celebrating an important anniversary or a lack of skills among the workforce. The type of need will depend on the policies, strategy and objectives of the investing organisation.

At this early stage, the work on the project is often largely theoretical. A proposal will be drawn up, describing what the project is designed to accomplish, and how (in broad terms) it will be done. If the idea looks promising, a feasibility study may be organised. This is a small scale investigation into the principles and methods to be used in the project.

At the start of a project, relatively few resources are required. A single individual, or a small team, can often do the preliminary work necessary to establish the viability of the project. By the end of this first stage, a decision will be taken to drop the project – or to take it on to the next phase in the life cycle.

Planning and organisation

Now the project manager makes detailed plans. These include a breakdown of all the tasks involved, a schedule and a budget. Specifications are produced for the resources required. Risks and contingencies are considered. Potential team members are approached and premises, equipment and suppliers are identified. Project management skills are essential at this stage. At the end of this phase, a project plan is produced and a decision is taken on whether the project should actually be made a reality.

Implementation

Now the project manager puts the plans into action. This is the time of maximum activity and resource use. At this stage, the project manager's role includes monitoring the work of the team and control of the budget and schedule. The implementation phase ends with the handover of the project outcome to the organisation which has invested in it.

The product could be:

- A residential building which is ready for occupancy

- A pharmaceutical product which can go into production

- A book which is ready for publication

- A training course which is ready for use within an organisation.

The exact point of handover will differ from situation to situation. For example, a project to develop a training course could end with the delivery of a set of videos and notes to be used by the organisation's in-house training department. In another situation, the training sessions could form part of the project and handover might occur when the project team delivered a report which described the skills development that had taken place.

Conclusion

At this point, the main project deliverable has been handed over. As far as many people are concerned, the project is now finished. However, the project manager still has some important work to do. The team must be disbanded, project documents must be assembled, reports must be drawn up and contracts checked and closed. There are also lessons to be learned. The project manager needs to reflect on every aspect of the project and consider what should be done differently another time around. The investing organisation will also want to consider the efficacy of the project. Were the original objectives achieved? Was it money well spent? Could more have been achieved? This final evaluation may have to wait for some time, until the long-term effects of the project can be assessed.

Although most projects follow this general pattern, in many cases the phases will be broken down into smaller sections. On many projects, the cycle of start-up, planning, implementation and conclusion happens several times, with each phase having the characteristics of a separate project. The types of skill needed at each stage may be different, and a new team may be appointed.

What were the phases of your last project called? How did they correspond to the design cycle?

Stakeholders

Many individuals and organisations have a stake in the success of a project. The most visible stakeholders are often the sponsors, or clients. The sponsoring organisation is the body which sets up the project and directs funds into it. If the project is a success, the organisation will benefit. The payoff it receives can take many forms. For example, the sponsoring organisation may obtain a commercial advantage over its rivals, an increase in sales, entry into a new market, public recognition, or perhaps the ability to attract funding and top rank staff for its next project. Of course, if the project goes badly, the sponsoring organisation may experience a drop in its competitiveness, sales and reputation. It may also find that its ability to attract funds for future projects has taken a serious knock.

The individuals within an organisation who have spoken up for a project also have a lot to gain – or lose. A senior manager, or, in the case of a national scheme, a government minister, whose name is associated with a particularly successful or unsuccessful project can find that his or her credibility and career prospects are either enhanced or damaged.

The sponsors of a project are important stakeholders and the project manager must take their views into account at all times. They can be powerful friends, willing to give extra support if they can be convinced that this is necessary to achieve the objectives of the project. They can also be powerful enemies. If sponsors fear that a project is about to fail, they may withdraw their support to safeguard their own reputation.

A project's sponsors are not, of course, the only people who have an interest. A project has an effect on the world. It makes a difference. Even a small internal project, such as the reorganisation of the filing system in an office, can be of enormous significance to the individuals who have to work with its results. A large project, such as the construction of a reservoir or the introduction of new educational standards, can completely change the lives of the local population and have a momentous effect on the social and economic future of the area. The people who are affected by the outcomes of a project can include the end users of a new product or service – and the staff of the organisation which provides that product or service. Local businesses and people who live in the area may also have a stake in the success of a project. And competitors can have a stake in the *failure* of a project.

The team which works on the project should also be considered as stakeholders. Their future careers will be affected, to a greater or lesser extent, by its success or failure. On a more personal level, the more the members of the team identify with the objectives of the project, the more effort and imagination they will contribute in order to make it succeed. Commitment brings a sense of ownership, which the project manager should treat with respect. There is also an unseen, but sometimes significant, group of stakeholders whom the project manager should not neglect. Many members of the project team can only function effectively at work because they have the support of their families. At the beginning of a project, this support may be gladly given. However, project managers who presume too much, by for example insisting on unnecessarily antisocial working arrangements, may find that this support is withdrawn and that some members of the team are not able to perform in the way they had hoped.

There may be other stakeholders, too:

'Last year I organised the production of some training materials. It sounds strange, but the individual on whom the project had most impact was the manager of the company's reprographic department. I put a great deal of work his way at a time when the future of his department was under threat. The work he did for me saved him from redundancy.'

Stakeholders can include contractors, suppliers, local pressure groups and, indeed, any organisation or individual who thinks they have something to gain, or lose, as a result of a project. It is important to identify the stakeholders in a project as early as possible, because these people can use their influence either to support or to block your efforts. When a project is announced, you may find that you have to add other stakeholders to your list. They may include individuals or groups whose interests you had not previously considered.

'When we announced that we were intending to build an industrial park on the outskirts of a small town, we thought the local population would be delighted by the prospect of more jobs. We did not know that there was an extremely vocal environmental group in the area which took it upon itself to oppose any new developments which would 'change the character' of the town.'

'We were surprised when the local Member of Parliament took such an interest in our work experience project. It turned out that she had long been a campaigner for more resources going into youth employment. She saw our project as a very positive development and wanted to be associated with it.'

As a project manager, you may find yourself coming under fire from people whom you think have no business to concern themselves with your project. However, if they consider themselves to be stakeholders, you ignore their views at your peril.

Meeting the expectations of stakeholders

It is important to establish what your stakeholders expect and do your best to meet these expectations. The requirements of the sponsor will be detailed in the Terms of Reference document which is prepared at the start of the project. Of course, your sponsor may also have other expectations, which are not specified here. Some of them may never be put in writing at all. Prior to the preparation of the Terms of Reference, there will undoubtedly have been some negotiation, either within the sponsoring organisation or as part of the tendering process, about what it is possible to achieve. It can be immensely useful if the project manager, or someone else who has genuine understanding and experience of the issues involved, is allowed to have an input into these preliminary discussions:

'I was approached by a company to design and introduce an information system. After our first meeting, I could tell that they wanted to reduce costs by doing as much as possible of the preliminary design work in-house. Basically,

they wanted to design their information system themselves, and then get me to computerise it for them. I had been in this situation before, and knew that it would be unlikely to result in a satisfactory outcome. My first job was to convince them that it would be better for an outside expert, such as myself, to undertake the design of the system. This would undoubtedly be more expensive, but would be a prudent investment.'

It is not uncommon for sponsors to have unrealistic objectives for a project. As a project manager, you should try to ensure that the objectives you take on are achievable. It is much better to do this at the start of a project, before major costs have been incurred. If you do not question the objectives, you may find that you are under contract to achieve the impossible – and that the responsibility for failure is laid at your door.

You must also be aware of the requirements of the stakeholders who will be affected by the project outcome. If, for example, you were working on a housing project, it would be important to have access to some detailed market research into the wishes of people who were actually going to live in the houses. Similarly, if you were developing a new magazine, you would need a profile of the intended readership. The more you know about the needs of end-users before you begin, the more likely you are to able to meet these needs.

Attention to the needs of end-users will affect the take-up of whatever it was that your project was set up to provide – and can also have an impact on how people feel about the project while it is underway. A project is much more likely to gain acceptance if people think that it is going to give them something that they want. It is also possible to overcome at least some of the resistance to a project by involving end-users in some of the decisions that have to be taken.

'I was asked to take on a project to advise on an organisation's relocation from their old offices in the city centre to a business park five miles away. The move was deeply unpopular and the company was worried that they would lose some of their key members of staff, which was why they brought me in. I couldn't give staff the easy access to the city centre pubs, shops and restaurants

that they visited in their lunchtimes, but I could help them develop a sense of ownership for their new offices. I did this by suggesting to senior management that everyone who moved was invited to help design their own workspace. People were allowed to choose their own desks, chairs, filing cabinets and workstations, from an approved range. They even decided the decor of the new offices. The cost to the organisation was minimal and soon the majority of staff were actually looking forward to the relocation.'

When stakeholders' needs conflict

You can't please all of the people all of the time. It is inevitable that some of the decisions you take as a project manager will be unpopular with some of the stakeholders. If you find that the needs of two groups of stakeholders conflict, it is advisable to give priority to the needs of customers. For example, if you were managing the construction of a new civic centre, you might want to use a local architect. However, if you felt that this architect was not capable of designing a building which would meet the requirements of the local people, you would be well advised to look further afield. If you have to make a choice, it is usually better to disappoint a supplier than a customer.

The customers for the end-product of the project may not be the same as the customers for the project itself. This situation can arise if the sponsors are paying for the project on behalf of another group. If you see a dichotomy developing between the expectations of the sponsor and the end-users, you can should anticipate difficulties ahead.

'Some years ago, I was asked to produce a leaflet giving contraceptive advice to young people. The charity which commissioned me had done a lot of work in the field and had strong ideas on what it wanted to communicate. They wanted something which young people in the target group could identify with and would not dismiss as 'just another piece of propaganda'. I went out of my way to use vocabulary which the audience would understand. The charity was delighted with what I produced. However, when we piloted the leaflet in schools, teachers and parents condemned it as 'corrupting' and 'pornographic'. The

sponsors of the project had lost touch with what was acceptable to some of their most important stakeholders.'

As a project manager, you have a responsibility to achieve the outcome that the sponsor is expecting. This can be problematic if you believe that this outcome will not be acceptable to the end-users. If you say nothing, you may find at the end of the project that 'the operation was a success, but the patient died.' The best course of action is to try to convince the sponsors, at as early a moment as possible, of the difficulties that you see, so that they can decide whether they want to revise their expectations.

Action Checklist

- *Who are your stakeholders?*

- *What are their expectations?*

- *What harm can they do you?*

- *What support can they give you?*

- *Will you be able to meet all their expectations?*

- *If not, what are you going to do?*

Time, cost and quality

These three issues are sometimes referred to as the 'eternal triangle' of project management. Your brief as a project manager is to deliver:

- On schedule

- Within budget

- To specification.

You must quantify and agree these three dimensions of the project at the start, and monitor them as the project progresses. However, dilemmas can arise because of the complicated interrelationships between time, cost and quality. In some situations, you may have to sacrifice the budget to the schedule, or the schedule and the budget to the specification. The decision about which of these three elements has priority will depend on the nature of the project – and the views of the sponsor.

Time

A project is made up of a sequence of interrelated activities. If you are making a film, you cannot start shooting until you have chosen your actors, arranged your locations and prepared your script. You cannot edit your footage until you have shot it. You cannot add music until you have recorded the score and produced a final cut of your picture. One task is dependent on the completion of another. It is from dependencies such as these that the work is planned and scheduled.

A delay in any of these individual tasks can put the whole schedule at risk. A week's delay in completing your script can mean that the location you want to use is not available. You may have to wait another four weeks before you are allowed access to it. By this time, your leading actor may be under contract to appear in a television commercial in Australia, and shooting has to be postponed until he returns in two weeks' time. Before you know it, a delay of one week in completing the script has resulted in a delay of seven weeks in the shooting schedule.

Key Management Concept

A delay in any part of a project can have serious knock-on effects on subsequent activities.

It is the project manager's responsibility to understand the dependencies within a project – and to do everything possible to ensure that those activities which are critical to the schedule happen when they are supposed to. In Chapter 3 we will examine some of the planning techniques you can use to do this.

In a project of any size, the schedule is punctuated by milestones. These are dates which mark the end of particular phases, or other significant events. Milestones provide interim goals and help you to measure your progress. They are also useful points at which to reflect on how things are going.

Cost

The longer a project goes on, the greater the costs are likely to be. Many variable costs, such as wages or hire of equipment, will be directly related to the time it takes to complete a project. If you get behind schedule, you may have to put in extra resources in order to meet a crucial deadline.

'The commercial success of our project depended on having our product in the shops by early November. We knew that most of our sales would come in the weeks before Christmas. At the end of September, we were four weeks behind schedule. I took the decision to take on extra staff to get the project finished on time. The cost was considerable, but the prospect of losing four weeks' sales was even worse.'

The time a project takes can affect costs in other ways, too. Some contracts include clauses which reward the contractors for prompt completion and penalise them for any delays. In a commercial project of any size, the original viability of the scheme will have been assessed on the basis of when revenues can be expected to come in. If this moment is significantly later than scheduled, the value of the cash received will be less.

When costs are paid out, they must be matched to the work they were intended to pay for. In some projects, interim payments are made at milestones, on delivery of particular elements. In other situations, the work is costed and scheduled and paid for at regular intervals. If the team is being paid on a time basis, it is particularly important to check the work that has actually been done against the work that was scheduled.

Quality

In management terminology, quality is not an abstract idea, like 'beauty' or 'goodness'. It means the extent to which something is 'fit for purpose'. There are two aspects to this fitness for purpose, both of which are important to the project manager. First of all, the end-product of the project must be capable of performing the function for which it is intended. This needs to be considered at the very start of a project. Specifications need to be agreed and set down in the Terms of

Reference. (It is also crucial that these specifications are agreed at a level which can realistically be met within the budget and timescale of the project.) Secondly, the project manager must consider the fitness for purpose, or quality, of all the interim deliverables which are produced on the way to the end-product. These can include planning documents, parts of a building construction, the outline of a book, or any individual component of a project.

One of the principles used in quality management is that it is unwise to wait until a process is finished before checking that the outcome is up to standard. Regular checks need to be performed on the inputs into the process, and on the process itself. This idea is perhaps even more important in project management, where you only have one opportunity to achieve your outcomes. When you plan a project, you therefore need to think very carefully about:

- The skills and experience of your team

- The specifications you require in your other resources

- The processes you will use

- The interim checks you will build into the implementation phase of the project.

All these things will impact on the time and cost of a project. Here is an example of how quality considerations affected the cost of a project:

'The company which asked me to produce a multimedia CD for its recruitment services suggested that I used part of an old training video to show the types of work it did. This material was hopelessly out of date, and of a poor technical quality. I insisted that they gave me a budget to shoot some new sequences for the CD. My argument was that if they were not prepared to spend this money, I would not be able to produce a CD which showed that they were at the cutting edge of the industry.'

And here is an example of how concerns about quality affected the schedule:

'I was involved in an advertising project whose objective was to change young people's attitudes to a particular commercial product. My agency came up with some excellent ideas, which we presented to the clients. They were so impressed that they wanted to get a TV advertising campaign underway immediately. I had to explain that we needed to take these ideas to the customer first. We had to organise focus groups of young people and then analyse the results. Sufficient time for this investigation had to be built into the schedule.'

- *What quality standards should you be working to?*

- *Are these standards achievable within the budget and timescale?*

- *How will you ensure that these standards are met?*

- *What impact will your quality assurance checks have on the budget and schedule?*

Action Checklist

Questions to reflect on and discuss

1. Think about an incident which happened when you were acting in the role of a project manager and something did not go as well as you had expected it would.

    Answer these questions about the incident:

    - What was the situation?

    - Who was involved?

    - What went wrong?

    - Why did it happen?

    - What were the consequences?

2. Now reflect on what this incident can tell you about your own learning needs in relation to project management. Could the incident have been

Activity

avoided, or its consequences have been less serious, if you had had greater:

- Knowledge of the theory of project management ?
- Knowledge and experience of planning and control techniques?
- Leadership skills?
- Technical knowledge of a specific area of work?
- Communication skills?
- Understanding of the needs of stakeholders?
- Understanding of the relationship between time, cost and quality?

3. Write two or three sentences outlining what you hope to gain by reading this book.

Early days

Chapter 2

This chapter examines what has to happen before a project gets underway. As a project manager, you may only become involved at the end of this stage. You may simply be presented with the Terms of Reference which are drawn up at the end of this phase and be asked to prepare a plan to put the project into action.

It is always an advantage if the project manager who will be responsible for carrying out a project is consulted during the preliminary discussions. If you are involved, you can use your previous experience to advise on whether the proposed working methods, resource levels and staffing arrangements are likely to be effective – and argue for what you believe is necessary. You should also be able to provide guidance on whether the scope of the project is too ambitious, or not ambitious enough.

It is also important for project managers to understand the past history of the projects on which they are working. Why is this project so important to the organisation? How does it relate to their overall strategy? Why was this project selected instead of another one? The answers to questions like these will help you to appreciate the priorities and concerns of your clients. This understanding can be of immense assistance during the implementation phase of the project, when it is essential for you to retain the confidence and support of the people who are paying the bills.

This chapter begins by considering the different ways in which projects can arise. Some are designed in response to an identified need, while in other circumstances the idea for the project precedes the perceived need. In either set of circumstances, the objectives of the project must be matched to those of the organisation which is investing in it. There are also other considerations which are taken into account when an idea for a project is evaluated. The financial viability of the project will invariably be considered. Most organisations will only give their support to projects which are in harmony with their own values and culture. And early consideration must also be given to the risks which are involved in a project.

This chapter also describes the process of issuing and responding to an Invitation to Tender – and looks at issues to consider when preparing a proposal. It goes on to examine the principles of negotiation and what you can do to reach a settlement which will enhance, and not damage, your relations with the people you will be working with on the project. It ends by describing the contents of the Terms of Reference document.

Where do projects come from?

Projects do not arise spontaneously. They are pulled or pushed into existence. A 'pulled' project is one which is commissioned by a sponsor in response to a perceived need. A 'pushed' project is one where the initial impetus comes from an organisation or an individual who wants the project to happen, but does not have the resources to sponsor it.

'Pulled' projects

In the first situation, the need precedes the project. The main priority is to establish that:

1. The project will achieve what it is intended to do.

2. It will do this better than any other proposed investment of time, cash and other resources.

It is usual for several alternative projects to be considered and evaluated – before the one which will meet the sponsor's objectives most effectively and efficiently is selected. The project manager may well be involved at this early stage and may help the sponsor to gather and evaluate this information.

When an organisation commissions a project, it is usually because:

• It has a problem, *or*

• It sees an opportunity it wants to exploit.

The problem or opportunity will, or at least should be, be directly related to the overall business strategy which the organisation is pursuing. There are five basic types of strategy which organisations can adopt:

- Maintaining or increasing sales of an existing product or service in an existing market
- Developing a new product or service for an existing market
- Taking an existing product or service to a new market
- Developing a new product or service for a new market
- Retrenchment.

Each one of these strategies can give rise to projects. Here are some examples of ways in which organisations have used projects:

Consolidating an existing market: *'Sales were falling and we were gradually losing our market share. We decided that we had to reduce our prices, which we could only achieve by making savings within the company. We commissioned a project to design a new information system which would enable us to increase efficiency and reduce staffing levels.'*

Developing a new product for an existing market: *'We set up a special team to design a new range of swimwear to complement the clothing we were already making for the 11-16 market.'*

Taking an existing product or service to a new market: *'We wanted to expand our operation by opening a chain of retail outlets in the major cities of Europe. We began by setting up a project team to come up with a concept which would be attractive to customers in Paris, Rome and Dublin.'*

Diversifying into a new market with a new product: *'We have an established business producing computer games for the leisure market. We decided to diversify into educational software and set up a project to* *design and develop a series of programs based on the National Curriculum for use in primary schools.'*

Retrenchment: *'We recently had to make over two hundred people redundant in one of our regional centres. We knew that the process would be extremely difficult for local management and brought in a specialised team of consultants to organise things and provide career counselling for those members of staff that wanted it.'*

Some shifts in strategy can be dealt with within the ordinary operational structure of an organisation. However, the more change that a strategy involves, the more likely an organisation is to set up a project.

Projects allow organisations to:

- Make changes without disturbing the underlying operation

- Bring in, or develop, new kinds of expertise

- Increase their capacity on a temporary basis.

'Pushed' projects

'Pushed' projects are frequently dreamed up by a single, innovative (and sometimes charismatic) individual. People like this often have a vision of something they would like to see happen in the future, but lack the resources to make it happen. Artistic projects, such as films and plays, major public events and construction projects, such as those planned to celebrate the Millennium, are all examples of 'pushed' projects. They can also arise inside organisations. You may know colleagues within your own organisation who are constantly trying to obtain backing for their projects. (You may even be one of these innovative individuals yourself.)

When someone has an idea for a project of this kind, the first priority is to identify potential sponsors and persuade them that the project is worth doing. This usually involves identifying an organisation with objectives which will be met by the project. For example, if you had an idea for a new product which could be made by people with the minimum of training and equipment and would produce a respectable profit, you might look for an organisation which was interested in supporting employment opportunities in an economically deprived area of the country. You could also approach a company which was already making a related product and which was interested in expanding its operations without investing vast sums in new machinery.

You need to start by doing some research. This may simply consist of some informal networking, or involve a series of more formal approaches to likely organisations or individuals. If a project is likely to result in financial gain, it is prudent not to give too many details away until you are convinced that the potential sponsor is seriously interested. In some circumstances, you may have to protect yourself by obtaining patents or by registering the copyright of your idea before approaching potential backers.

Useful questions to consider in relation to a potential sponsor:

- *What resources does this sponsor have at its disposal?*

Action Checklist

- *What kind of projects has this sponsor sponsored in the past?*

- *What other demands does this sponsor have on its resources?*

- *What is the current policy of the sponsor towards investment?*

- *What conditions is this sponsor likely to attach to sponsorship?*

Once you had identified a potential sponsor, you would have to demonstrate that your project would meet their objectives. You might also find that you were having to compete for funds against people who were pushing other projects.

The initial dynamics of these two situations are different. In the first case, the existence of the need for a project has already been accepted. The key decision is whether a particular project is the one that should go ahead. In the second situation, it is necessary to identify potential sponsors and to persuade them that the project is worth doing.

Evaluating a project

We will now consider the criteria which sponsors use when deciding whether to invest in a project. To begin with, a sponsoring organisation is only likely to look seriously at a project which is consistent with its overall strategy, values and culture. Here are some examples of projects which failed to pass these first hurdles:

'Someone came up with a proposal to increase turnover by refurbishing all the outlets in the south west region. However, it ran counter to our policy of gradually phasing out our operations in that part of the country. The project never stood a chance of acceptance.'

'We have a certain amount of money which we make available to local groups for projects which will improve the quality of urban life. We recently received a proposal from an organisation which wanted to establish a drop-in centre for people who work in the sex industry. In the projects we support, we try to emphasise the importance of family values and felt that this proposal was not consistent with what we were trying to achieve.'

'We asked several design companies to put in tenders for a project to produce a new look for our retail outlets. One idea involved going over to self service. Since we pride ourselves on the high level of individual attention we give to our customers, many of whom are very traditional in their outlook, we felt that this idea was inappropriate.'

In some situations, a particularly innovative and exciting project proposal may succeed in changing the sponsor's underlying strategy, values or culture, but this does not happen very often. Decisions about the general direction in which the sponsoring organisation is heading are usually taken before it considers proposals for projects and are difficult to reverse.

Assessing the financial viability of a project

Before committing itself to a project, an organisation needs to be confident that it is making a wise financial decision. If the project is designed to produce income in the future, the amount and timing of this revenue will need to be calculated. These figures may need to be prepared and presented by someone with specialised financial training. The costs of a project also need to be calculated.

Once an organisation knows how much a project is likely to cost, and how much money it is likely to bring in, it can compare these figures with those for other competing investments, or with a benchmark. There are several techniques which organisations use to evaluate investments:

- Pay-back

- Discounted pay-back

- Accounting rate of return

- Net present value

- Internal rate of return.

We will give an outline of each of these methods. In practice, the calculations are likely to be done by financial specialists. However, it is extremely useful to understand the basis on which a project will be evaluated by potential investors.

Pay-back

The simplest way to evaluate an investment is to look at the time it will take to pay for itself. A project which costs £1,000,000 and which will generate income of £100,000 in the first year, £400,000 in the second year and £500,000 in the third year has a pay-back period of three years. Another project which costs £1,000,000 and which will bring in £200,000 a year for the foreseeable future has a pay-back period of five years.

If the two investments were equally attractive in other ways, an organisation using the pay-back method would select the one which has the shorter pay-back period. Other organisations set a limit, of for example three years, and do not consider investments with a longer pay-back period.

The advantage of the pay-back method is that it is easy to understand. There are also some major disadvantages to this method of evaluation. In the first place, it takes no account of what happens after the pay-back period. Common sense tells us that it is better to choose an investment which will continue to produce income for a longer period. Another significant difficulty is that this method takes no account of when income is due to come in.

Discounted pay-back

In business, money has a time value. Any funds which an organisation holds are not left to sit idly in a safe, but are put to work. This means that £1 which you have now is worth more than £1 which will arrive at some date in the future. Let's suppose that you invest your money in an enterprise which will bring in 10 per cent interest a year. At the end of 12 months, £1 has become £1.10.

$$£1.00 \times \frac{110}{100} = £1.10$$

You can also do this calculation backwards and work out that £1.10 which you receive in a year's time is only worth £1 which you have now.

$$£1.10 \times \frac{100}{110} = £1.00$$

Taking the same rate of interest of 10 per cent, you can look at any amount which you will receive in the future and calculate its equivalent value in money which you have today:

$$£1,000 \times \frac{100}{110} = £909$$

£1,000 which you receive in a year's time is only worth £909 at present value, assuming an interest rate of 10 per cent.

If cash is invested for a longer period of time, its present value is even smaller:

$$£1,000 \times \frac{100}{110} \times \frac{100}{110} = £826$$

The discounted pay-back method reduces the money which will come in from an investment to its present value. It takes account of the fact that £1,000 which arrives in two years' time is worth less than £1,000 which arrives in one year's time. This gives a much better indication of the value of an investment. However, this method still does not take into account any income after the pay-back period is over.

Accounting rate of return

This method involves taking the average profits of the investment and dividing them by the average book value. The 'average book value' is a piece of accounting terminology. It means the figure which is obtained by deducting depreciation from the initial cost of an investment.

Although many organisations use this method to evaluate investments, it has certain significant disadvantages. Firstly, it requires some knowledge of how financial statements are prepared. Secondly, like the pay-back method, it does not take into account the time value of money. Profits are averaged out over several years, so projects which would produce profits more quickly than others are not given priority. Thirdly, this method is based on figures for profit, not cash flow. In a situation where there is a long delay between issuing an invoice and receiving payment, the impression created by this method of evaluation could be very misleading.

Net Present Value

This method of evaluation is similar to the discounted pay-back method. It looks at the opportunity costs of the capital involved. These are equal to the market interest rate for investments which carry a similar risk. The Net Present Value method works by comparing cash outflow today with cash inflows in the future which are discounted at a rate equivalent to the opportunity costs. For example, if shareholders could expect a 10 per cent return on their money if they invested it on the open market, future inflows of cash would be discounted at 10 per cent per annum.

Unlike discounted pay-back, this method takes into account cash inflows over the whole life of the investment, not just the pay-back period. It also brings into the equation the terminal value of a project – any cash that can be realised by selling off equipment, premises or other assets when the project is over. Net

Present Value has many advantages. It is not significantly more complicated to calculate than discounted pay-back and it produces much more useful results.

Internal rate of return

You may also come across organisations which use this method of evaluating investments. It involves comparing the present cash outflows and the future cash inflows of a project and working out what the rate of return would have to be in order for these figures to be equal. (You can perform this calculation using a computer spreadsheet.) The rate of return will appear as a percentage, which can then be compared with a pre-determined 'hurdle' which the organisation has set for all its investments, or with the rate of return promised by another project. The higher the rate of return, the more profitable an investment is likely to be. The disadvantage of this method is that it gives a percentage figure, not an absolute amount. This can distort decision-making. For example, there are circumstances where it would be better to invest in a large project with a slightly lower rate of return than in a smaller, more limited project, with a higher rate.

As a project manager, you probably will not be involved in evaluating the viability of investments. You should, however, be aware of the facts that the sponsors have taken into account when making their decision to invest. This could be important if you have to negotiate changes to the budget, schedule or scope of the project once it is underway.

What's the risk?

The sponsors of a project need to know the level of risk that they are taking. As the individual in charge of a project, you also need to know which elements of it are most critical to its success. One way to consider risk is to perform a sensitivity analysis.

A sensitivity analysis is a method of looking at the components of a budget forecast and calculating the percentage by which they would have to change to make the project unprofitable.

Key Management Concept

When you produce the budget for a project, you will estimate figures for the various costs involved. These may include:

- Purchase of equipment

- Hire of premises

- Salaries and wages

- Raw materials.

If your project is designed to generate income, you will also need to calculate how much cash you expect to come in, and when it will arrive. These figures will be based on the volume of sales you expect to make, and the price at which goods or services will be sold.

In an ideal world, your actual costs and income will match your estimates exactly. In the real world, things will probably work out slightly differently. If you run into difficulties and the project takes longer to complete than you expected, you may have to pay more in labour costs. If the service you are offering turns out not to be as popular with customers as you had hoped, your income will be lower than estimated.

A sensitivity analysis takes each item on a budget forecast and calculates the percentage by which that figure would have to change to make the total discounted cash inflow from the project less than the cash outflow. In so doing, it highlights the critical figures on the budget forecast.

For example, let us suppose that you are working on a two year project which will derive its income from the sales of specialised multimedia CDs to businesses. In the first year you aim to produce five CDs, the sales of which will finance the second year of development. The marketing research has suggested that you could sell 100 copies each of these five CDs, at a unit price of £200. You expect to make these sales during the second year of the project. There are several things which could go wrong with this plan:

- You might produce fewer than five CDs in your first year

- You might sell fewer copies than you expected

- It might take longer for the CDs to sell

- The people you have employed to work on the CDs might not be as skilled as you expected – you might have to replace them with more expensive staff

- Your premises might be burgled repeatedly – you might have to pay more for insurance or pay for extra security

- A competitor might bring out a similar product at a lower price.

Some of these things could have a disastrous effect on your project, while others would not be so serious. A sensitivity analysis might show you that you could afford to increase your security costs by 150 per cent without endangering the profitability of the project. On the other hand, if your wage bill forms a large part of your budget, you may only be able to pay 5 per cent more on this item. The lower the percentage figure, the more crucial this item is to the success of the project.

This information will be of use to the potential sponsors. If it appears that there are items on the budget which are critical to the success of the project and which are also likely to change, they will be unwilling to invest. A sensitivity analysis will also help you, as the project manager, to decide which areas of the budget you need to protect. It will also help you to think about your priorities if you have to modify your plans when the project is underway.

There are, of course, several methods of dealing with risk. These need to be considered and costed in the early stages of a project, before the budget is agreed. In essence, you can:

- Take action in advance to avoid the risk, *or*

- Take action in advance to mitigate the effects of the risk, *or*

- Wait until a problem happens, and then take action to mitigate its effects, *or*

- Transfer the risk to another party, such as an insurance company or a sub-contractor.

We can apply these approaches to the situation described in the previous example. Imagine that you, in your role as multimedia producer, realise that it is crucial to the success of your project that the expected sales revenue is received early in the second year. If this cash does not arrive, funds will not be able to finance the second stage of development. There are several ways you could approach this risk.

- You could **take action in advance to avoid the risk** by funding a major marketing campaign. This could involve arranging pre-payment by customers at a discount. Alternatively, you could obtain funding for the full length of the project.

- You could **take action in advance to mitigate the effects of the risk** by employing staff on short contracts. If the hoped-for sales do not happen, the second development phase can be put on hold. In doing this, you would be laying yourself open to another risk. If you do not employ staff for the full length of the project, you may find it difficult to retain, or re-employ, key members of your team for the second phase.

- You **could wait until a problem happens, and then take action to mitigate its effects**, by doing nothing about the risk at the start of the project. If sales do not meet your expectations, you will then have to find a method of increasing revenue or lowering costs. This would be an unwise path to follow unless you have some evidence which suggests that the risk is very unlikely to happen.

- You could **transfer the risk to another party** by making a deal with a distribution company, selling your entire output (or a large proportion of it) in advance at a lower price.

Almost all ways of managing risk cost money and must be budgeted for at the start of the project. Even if you decide to do nothing in advance to protect yourself against a risk – which is a viable alternative if the risk is unlikely to happen – you must have some money in your budget to cover contingencies.

Key Question

How much of the success of a project is due to good luck? And how much is due to good risk management?

Invitation to Tender

When an organisation has a project which it wants to place with an outside contractor, it will often send out an Invitation to Tender (ITT). This is a document which asks interested suppliers to show that they can meet the requirements of the sponsoring organisation.

Before it issues an ITT, an organisation needs to do some preparatory work. It must consider:

- How the project will further the strategy of the organisation

- The project objectives – exactly what it wants to achieve by the project

- The financial and other resource implications of the project

- The timescale for the project

- The criteria it will use for selecting a contractor.

If the project is on a relatively small scale, or is very similar to an earlier project which the organisation has commissioned, it may be possible for senior management to settle these issues amongst themselves. If the project contains some new elements, the organisation will need expert advice on what is practicable. They may consult independent authorities at this point, or approach potential suppliers for this advice. And if the project involves a major investment in a new area, the organisation may set up a full-blown feasibility study.

An organisation may make informal enquiries to find out who is likely to be able to take on a project and then approach only these companies or individuals. Alternatively, it may choose to advertise its intentions in the press. Where public money is involved, there is sometimes a duty to open the tendering process to anyone who is interested.

An Invitation to Tender should contain this information:

- The objectives for the project

- Background information on the commissioning organisation

- Criteria for selection

- An outline of the project deliverables which are required

- A detailed timescale for the tendering process (issue of ITT, preliminary discussions, receipt of proposals, associated presentation of proposals, evaluation, award of contract)

- A timescale for the project itself

- The information required from the tendering organisation

- Format of the proposal.

The more details the organisation which issues the ITT can give about what it wants to know and how it wants this information presented, the easier it will find it to compare the proposals it receives.

Proposals

At the beginning of this chapter we said there were two kinds of projects: 'pulled' projects, which arise in response to a need recognised by the sponsors, and 'pushed' projects, where the original idea and impetus comes from a source other than the sponsor. There are certain differences in the way that proposals for these two types of project are prepared. However, there are also some important similarities, which we will look at first.

Whatever type of project is being proposed, it is essential to show that it is designed to produce outcomes which are in line with the objectives laid down by the sponsor. In the case of a commissioned project, detailed objectives may be included in the Invitation to Tender. In other circumstances, a funding body may set more general objectives in relation to the projects it is willing to consider.

It is also necessary to convince potential sponsors that the project is viable. This may be a question of supplying information which is requested in the Invitation to Tender, or of producing a business plan. The sponsor will need to know that you have considered:

Action Checklist

- The objectives of the project

- The potential market for the product or service

- How the product or service would be produced

- Some evidence of the feasibility of this process

- The costs and income involved, and the times at which they will arise

- How the project would be managed

- Any risks and problems associated with the project, and how they would be managed.

The level of detail included at this stage will vary greatly, according to the size of the investment involved and the demands of the sponsor. However, any details you provide are likely to undergo thorough scrutiny by experienced and knowledgeable individuals within the sponsoring organisation. Your plans must stand up to analysis.

When you are putting forward a proposal, it can be helpful to remember that the individuals who control finances do not always have much technical knowledge of the project area. They may not be able to interpret drawings or evaluate research data. You need to present your concept in a way which they can understand and which demonstrates, as far as is possible, the finished effect you want to achieve. Depending on the type of project you are promoting, you might present an architect's model of a building, a sample chapter of a book, a prototype of an invention, a demo tape of a piece of music or a set of projected sales figures. Showing your sponsors what will be achieved with their money is often a good way of gaining their commitment, whether you are putting forward a proposal in response to an Invitation to Tender, or trying to gain sponsorship for a concept of your own.

Key Question

Think about the last project you worked on. What convinced the sponsors to back it?

If you are preparing a proposal in response to an Invitation to Tender, it is essential to follow the instructions exactly. Proposals which are received after the due date, or do not give the details which are asked for, will probably not be considered at all. If you feel that the format of the proposal does not allow you to communicate everything you want to, it is often possible to add extra information.

Key Learning Point

Put everything you need to say in your written proposal. The people who read it may not have been privy to any preliminary meetings or informal conversations you had with the sponsor.

If you are trying to gain sponsorship for a project you are pushing, you may have to work a little harder. You have to convince sponsors that a situation exists which they ought to do something about and that your project, among all the courses of action they could adopt, is the best way forward. One approach you can use in this kind of proposal is to:

1. Start by describing the current position:
   'x thousand mousetraps are sold in the UK every year. The market is dominated by company A and company B...'

2. Next, describe the problem or opportunity which exists:
   'The mouse population has been rising by y per cent a year since 19XX, yet sales of mousetraps have remained static in the UK. We believe this is because of a growing repugnance among customers for the traditional mousetrap. A market research survey, conducted on our behalf, reported that 79 per cent of consumers regarded the traditional mousetrap as inhumane. A market opportunity exists for a more acceptable mousetrap...'

3. Then describe the possibilities for action, giving the advantages and disadvantages of each option. The more objective you can be at this stage, the more confident your readers are likely to be in the proposal which follows.

'It is possible to buy a 'humane mousetrap' which traps the mouse without killing it. This has the major disadvantage of making it necessary to dispose of the living mouse in a place where it will not re-infest the building... Our design for the 'Beta Mousetrap' has the advantage of anaesthetising the mouse and then eliminating it. Disposal of the remains is simple and hygienic, and the customer has the confidence that the mouse died happy...'

4. Make your proposal. It is important to recommend a clear course of action. Think of all the aspects your readers will be interested in, such as time, cost, resources, and answer any obvious objections.

'With an investment of £X,000, we can put the Beta Mousetrap into production within six months. The prototype has already received a safety certificate. Anticipated sales figures in the first 12 months would total £Y,000...'

This same technique can be used effectively in a face-to-face presentation.

Presenting a proposal

Everyone can learn the skills involved in giving a presentation, but it is undeniable that some people have a greater natural aptitude in this area than others. In Chapter 4 we discuss the different personalities that are needed in a team. Frequently the best person to give a presentation that will inspire and convince potential sponsors is the 'resource investigator'. This person is an excellent communicator, with a great deal of energy and enthusiasm, especially in the early stages of a project. If you are not a 'resource investigator' yourself, you may be able to hand the responsibility for giving a presentation to someone who is, or at least arrange to share the platform with him or her.

Presentations are usually delivered on the sponsors' premises. You need to find out in advance:

- Who you will be speaking to

- Who else will be speaking

- How long you have available for your presentation

- The layout of the room – and whether you will be able to prepare it

- The facilities for using audio visual aids.

When you plan your presentation, it is important to consider how you will keep the attention of your audience. People's interest usually decreases after the first ten minutes and only returns when they think you are reaching the end.

How to keep your audience interested:

- *Have a clear structure to your presentation*

- *Remind your audience where you are in your structure*

- *Don't read from a script – use prompts on cards*

- *Practise what you are going to say*

- *Make eye contact with your audience*

- *Use visual aids such as prepared flip charts, demonstrations and OHPs to vary your delivery.*

Action Checklist

A presentation is also an opportunity for sponsors to question you about your proposal. Try to anticipate as many difficult questions as you can, and prepare your answers in detail. Your audience will be impressed if they believe that you have already considered all the potential difficulties that they can come up with.

Negotiating for what you need

In the early stages of a project, when contracts are being arranged, you are very likely to be involved in negotiations. You may have to negotiate with the sponsor about how the project will be organised and resourced, or perhaps the terms on which it will be financed. You may also have to negotiate with sub-contractors and suppliers to obtain the resources you need to carry out the work.

Key Management Concept

A negotiation is a discussion in which the parties involved have different objectives.

Negotiations often centre around price. They can also be concerned with issues of time and quality. Very frequently, negotiations are really about questions of control.

'I was having a meeting with the departmental manager of someone who was seconded to my project team. We were trying to agree the number of days that this team member would spend working on the project. The manager wanted to allow me two days a week, throughout the project, making a total of 60 days. I said that wouldn't work, because there wasn't anything for this person to do in the first weeks of the project. However, at a later stage, I would need much more of her time. I thought that a total of 75 days, weighted towards the end of the project, was more realistic. We were arguing about a day here and a day there, and things began to get a little heated. Then something clicked. I realised that the real issue wasn't the number of days that this person would be working on the project. In any case, a temporary replacement from an agency would be brought in to cover her duties, at the project's expense. What the departmental manager was really worried about was the fact that there were some weeks in which I wanted the member of staff to work for me full time. He was concerned that his own line manager would think that he could run the department with a temporary replacement in this post, and this would diminish his own authority.'

Negotiations can end in one of three ways:

- WIN-LOSE: One side achieves its objectives, while the other side does not

- LOSE-LOSE: Neither side achieves their objectives

- WIN-WIN: Both sides achieve enough of their objectives to be satisfied with the result.

For some people, winning is all that matters. Their only concern in a negotiation is to achieve their own objectives. However, this is an extremely short-sighted approach. If you have ever been on the losing side in a negotiation, you will know that it is not a pleasant experience. You may have felt undermined, undervalued and out-manoeuvred. You may have felt angry about the treatment you received – and determined to prove yourself right on the first possible occasion.

'I told the managing director that Jerry was the person I wanted on the project team, but he went ahead and appointed Richard. I was absolutely furious about this. And I have to admit that, as a result, my attitude to Richard was not entirely positive. Instead of giving him the support he needed, I found myself letting him struggle on, in the hope that he would make a bad mistake and I could move him off the team.'

If you begin a working relationship with feelings of anger or resentment, this can distort the decisions that you make in the future. There are also dangers in coming out on the winning side:

'I managed to beat a supplier down to a very good price. He was not happy, but agreed to the contract. Some weeks in, I realised that I had made a mistake with the specification for some of the raw materials and needed to vary the order. When I telephoned the supplier, he said 'Sorry, I'm afraid I can't help you. It's not in the contract.' Game, set and match, as they say. He made me pay a hefty surcharge for a change which didn't really cost him anything at all to make.'

If you make someone into a loser in a negotiation, you may forfeit their goodwill. It is extremely important that everyone involved is able to accept the agreements which are reached at the beginning of a project. This usually means reaching a WIN-WIN outcome to negotiations, with which both sides can be reasonably satisfied.

In a negotiation, you may not get everything you want. Try to work out:

- Your ideal outcome – the best you hope to achieve

- Your realistic outcome – what you think you could reasonably expect to achieve

- Your fall-back position – the outcome you could live with, if you really had to.

In some situations, you may be prepared to walk away from the negotiations altogether. If you are able to approach another supplier, or even another potential sponsor, you are in a very strong position.

The art of bargaining involves showing as little of your own hand as possible, while trying to find out what cards your opponent holds. It is also a game of give and take.

The rules of bargaining:

1. Don't give anything without taking something in return.

2. Give things you can afford to lose.

3. Only take things you want to have.

These rules are useful to remember, especially if you are being pressured to make concessions which you don't want to make. However, their disadvantage is that they reinforce an adversarial model of negotiation, in which the other side are seen as opponents, not as potential partners. There are times when you need to abandon this model, and look for another way forward.

Action Checklist

Avoiding conflict in negotiations

Conflict makes negotiations more difficult to resolve. If tempers become raised, participants will find it hard to back down and accept a compromise solution. It is useful to begin a negotiation by both sides stating their position. The person who is leading the discussion can then make a quick assessment of where the areas of agreement and conflict are likely to be. It is usually a good idea to discuss the non-controversial areas first. In this way, commitment to the negotiations can be developed, before being tested on difficult issues.

It is never advisable to indulge in verbal attacks on the people you are negotiating with. If people are attacked, they will defend themselves by counter-attacking, and a downwards spiral of attack and defence will begin. If you find yourself under attack, try not to rise to the bait. In your response, make an effort to separate facts from opinions:

> **Senior manager:** *I suppose you will be expecting the company to pay for a state-of-the-art computer for the project team to amuse themselves with in their lunch breaks?*

> **Project manager:** *I have included the cost of a PC in the budget. We can get the machine we need for £1,200, plus VAT.*

> **Senior manager:** *Why can't you use the computer that's been sitting in the back office for the last two years? That was another monumental waste of money.*

> **Project manager:** *We need a machine with certain specifications to run the software we will be using. The minimum requirements are a Pentium 133Mhz with 32Mb of RAM and a 1.7 Gb hard drive.*

> **Senior manager:** *And the computer in the back room doesn't have those specifications?*

> **Project manager:** *No, I took a look at it last week. It's a 286 with a black and white monitor.*

> **Senior manager:** *Ah, I see what you mean.*

Getting past deadlock

You may reach a position where both sides are insisting on apparently incompatible demands. At this point, the negotiations are in danger of breaking down completely.

The best way to find a solution, if a solution exists, is to look for areas of common ground and build upon them.

This is how the project manager who was quoted earlier in this section found an answer to his problem with the departmental manager who was unwilling to release a member of staff at the times when she was needed:

'We had reached deadlock. I had one set of days which I wanted the individual to work on the project, and the departmental manager had a completely different set of days. I had to step back and look at the situation from a new perspective.

The thing that we both had in common was that we actually wanted the member of staff concerned to be involved in the project. I then thought, 'OK, what do we both have to do in order to make this possible?' My priority was to be able to use the individual when I needed her. The departmental manager's priority was not to give the impression that he could run the department with an inexperienced person in this post.

What I suggested was that, in the weeks when I required it, the member of staff would work for the project full time, but she would spend half an hour at the end of each day briefing and debriefing her temporary replacement. The departmental manager was happy with this arrangement, because he could use it to convince his superiors of the importance of the member of staff's work to his department.'

Sometimes, all that is needed is a change of emphasis. Instead of concentrating on the areas where you disagree, look for areas of agreement. Try to think what each side could offer to make it possible for the other side to achieve what it wants from the situation.

The art of persuasion

When you are trying to persuade someone to accept your point of view, it is important to consider things from their perspective. Think about what they want from the situation. Some of these objectives will be clearly stated in the negotiations or the accompanying documentation. Others will be unspoken, but no less real.

If you can get inside the minds of the people you are negotiating with, it is a great advantage. You do not have to be a psychic, or even a psychologist, to do this. You can learn a great deal from observation and common sense, for example:

- What can you learn about the prevailing culture from the premises an organisation occupies, the way people dress, how they talk to each other and the kind of letters they write? This will tell you about their priorities. A conservative culture will be less ready to take risks and may insist on more formal arrangements for a project.

- Is there a particular issue, which seems unimportant to you, that the other side keeps mentioning? Is this perhaps an area where they have had difficulties in the past? If so, they will need extra reassurance from you here.

Once you know what the other side wants, you must convince them that you can provide it. One way to do this is to provide a 'vision' of what you will achieve. This may be done by powerful speaking, or by some sort of demonstration or model of the project outcomes. It is also extremely useful to show that you have achieved similar things in the past.

In advertising leaflets, you often see lists of reasons why you should buy a particular product or service. It is sometimes appropriate to summarise the benefits of your proposal in a similar way:

'Our exciting and groundbreaking design for the civic centre will be an architectural landmark. People will come from all over Europe to see it for themselves. This will attract extra spending to the town and revitalise local businesses...'

However, if you can, it is often more effective if you leave something to people's imagination. Let them work out some of the benefits for themselves. For example, an artist's impression of a dramatic, new civic centre surrounded by prosperous-looking pavement cafés may make people think about the value of a design which would bring visitors into the area. This is obviously a technique which needs to be used with care. You have to know something about your audience to be able to predict what you have to spell out for them and what they will work out for themselves.

If you have assembled several arguments in favour of a proposal it is best not to present them all at once. Inevitably, some of your arguments will be stronger than others. If people can pick holes in the weaker parts of your case, your whole proposal will lose credibility. Also, if you present too many reasons why a particular course of action should be taken, people may begin to get a little suspicious. They will start looking for the catch. Present your best arguments first, and only bring in your secondary arguments if they are needed.

Terms of Reference

At the end of negotiations, a document is produced which describes the project in some detail. This document is usually known as the Terms of Reference. It forms the basis of the contract between the client and the contractor and is the cornerstone on which all subsequent decisions are based.

The Terms of Reference document usually contains the following information:

- The client

- The contractor

- The end-users of the project

- The project objectives

- The project deliverables

- The costs involved in the project

- The resources required

- The timescale

- The risks and contingencies.

The client

This is the organisation which has commissioned or sponsored the project. Frequently, a brief description is included, drawing attention to the overall mission or policy of the organisation. The roles and responsibilities of the client will be described here.

The contractor

This section names the team or organisation which will carry out the project and describes its roles and responsibilities. The individual roles of team members may be detailed, or simply what is expected of the team as a whole.

The end-users

These are the final customers for the product or service which will result from the project. The end-users may be the client organisation, or another group entirely. It is important that this group is identified right from the start, so that that their requirements can be taken into account.

Action Checklist

The project objectives

This section describes exactly what the project is designed to achieve. The objectives should be SMART:

- **S**imple

- **M**easurable

- **A**chievable

- **R**ealistic

- **T**ime-related.

The clearer the objectives are, the easier it is to check whether they have been met. Once the objectives have been established, it is all too easy to allow them to lie neglected and unread in the Terms of Reference document. Instead, they should be widely distributed throughout the project team, providing a focus for subsequent decisions.

The project deliverables

These are the tangible, physical items which the contractor will deliver to the client. The final project deliverable can be a building, a computer program, a set of training manuals, a bridge or perhaps a production model for a motor cycle. The final deliverable can also be a document which gives important information. It could, for example, be the report of a research survey or a procedure for manufacturing a chemical compound.

In addition to the final deliverable, there will also be other deliverables, to be handed over at various stages of the project. These could include a detailed project plan, briefing notes for the project team, results of safety checks or pilot studies or perhaps a set of architect's drawings. These deliverables will confirm that the project has been administered satisfactorily. The end of each stage in a project is usually marked by the handover of some kind of deliverable.

Sometimes, the project objectives and the project deliverables are both described together in a section describing the scope of a project.

The costs

Where a project is to be carried out by an outside contractor, this figure will represent the fee which has been agreed with the client. Where a project is to be carried out internally, the figure will represent the expected cost of performing all the activities involved. A considerable amount of work may have gone into this calculation, with each item costed separately. On the other hand, it is sometimes impossible to work out a precise figure at this early stage of a project and the amount included here may be based on experience of past projects and some educated guesswork. Chapter 3 describes the principles of estimating. Any deviation from the costs given in the Terms of Reference will have to be agreed by both parties at a later stage.

The resources

This section describes the personnel, equipment, raw materials, information and other resources necessary to complete the project. It will be linked to the section dealing with costs.

The timescale

Here, the overall schedule is given. The dates of important milestones, marking the end of particular stages in the project, are established.

The risks and contingencies

This section lists any significant risks which have been identified and outlines how the project will be protected against them. These risks and contingencies will be further investigated during the detailed planning stage.

Questions to reflect on and discuss

Activity

1. Think of a project you would like to work on at some time in the future. Describe it briefly, then answer the following questions:

    •   Who could commission this project?

    •   What financial and other criteria would they use when evaluating it?

    •   Approximately how much would the project cost?

    •   Approximately how long would it take?

    •   What risks would be involved in the project, and how would you protect yourself against them?

2. Now use the guidance in this chapter to draft an outline proposal for your project.

Planning a project

Chapter 3

A large amount of the work of the project manager is concerned with making plans. There are special techniques which make this process easier. Many of these project management tools are now available in the form of computer software, but it is also important to understand the principles on which they work.

This chapter begins by examining the various ways in which one task can dependent on another. These relationships can be represented in flowcharts, network diagrams and Gantt charts. The work breakdown structure is also introduced. This document is central to the planning – and control – of a project.

However sophisticated the visual appearance of your plans, they will only be as valuable as the data on which they are based and the assumptions which you make. This chapter also discusses the principles of preparing budgets and schedules and of obtaining realistic estimates.

Planning and control are two sides of the same coin. The planning tools you select, and the way you use them, are crucial to the effectiveness of your monitoring system. By the end of this chapter, you should have a good understanding of the issues which are at stake.

Dependencies

Key Management Concept

A dependency is an activity which is connected to other activities.

In any project, there will be some things which cannot happen until other things have been accomplished. The dependencies which you build into your plan may be:

- Internal or external

- Mandatory or discretionary.

Internal dependencies are ones in which all the activities involved are under the control of the project manager. A simple example would be the mailing of a questionnaire which clearly cannot happen until the questionnaire has been printed.

External dependencies occur when project activities depend on something outside the project. For example, if a project cannot proceed unless it receives a grant from the National Lottery Fund, it is impossible to hire the staff and order the equipment until you know whether or not the grant application has been successful. It might, however, be possible to go ahead with other aspects of the project which do not require a major financial investment while you were waiting for the decision about the grant.

Mandatory dependencies are unavoidable. They often involve physical constraints. For example, you cannot tile the sides of a swimming pool before you have excavated the hole. You cannot test a computer program before you have designed it. Some dependencies, however, may not be as unavoidable as they appear:

'You may have thought that it was impossible to take publicity photographs of an encyclopaedia before it is printed. But if we waited until we had printed copies before we started our publicity, sales would be delayed unacceptably. We mock up a few pages in advance and photograph them for our leaflets.'

Discretionary dependencies, as the name suggests, are decided on the discretion of the project manager. He or she may decide to follow a standard procedure (if such a procedure exists) or, if there are specific reasons for doing things differently on a particular project, to depart from this standard way of organising activities.

'We normally complete the fitting of the kitchens and bathrooms before we pass our houses over to the sales department. However, we decided on this occasion to make a special selling point of the fact that buyers could choose their own cabinets and bathroom suites. This meant that the fitting had to wait until the houses were sold.'

If any of your dependencies are discretionary, it is important to document the decisions you have made. This helps you remember that you had a choice about these matters and allows you to change your mind if circumstances alter.

Key Management Concept

It is often easier to identify dependencies by working backwards. Think about the end result you want to achieve, then consider what has to be done before this can happen.

The most common form of dependency is for the start of one activity to be dependent on the finish of another. This is known as a finish-to-start dependency. It may be possible for the second activity to start as soon as the first has finished, or there may be a time lag. For example, the walls of a house cannot be painted until they are plastered. However, painting cannot take place immediately after plastering – it must wait until the plaster has been allowed to cure.

Three other types of dependency also occur quite commonly:

- Start-to-finish – where an activity cannot finish before another activity has started, or there is a known time relationship between the start of one activity and the finish of another

- Finish-to-finish – where activities must finish at the same time, or there is a known time relationship between the finish of the activities

- Start-to-start – where activities must start at the same time, or there is a known time relationship between the start of the two activities.

An example of a start-to-finish dependency could be the production of business cards for the project team and the installation of telephones. Although the design of the cards can be settled, the details cannot be finalised until telephone numbers have been allocated. The finish of the activity 'producing business cards' therefore has to wait until the start of the activity 'installing telephones'.

A finish-to-finish dependency could be the transport of a celebrity speaker to a presentation and the entry and seating of the audience. If either the speaker or the audience has to wait too long, the success of the presentation is jeopardised. An example of a start-to-start dependency could be the excavation of a tunnel and the reinforcing of the roof.

Flowcharts

A flowchart is a diagram which depicts a sequence of interdependent activities.

Flowcharts are used in ordinary, operational management to examine processes and look for more effective methods of doing them. In project management, they can be used to map out the general shape of what needs to be done.

In essence, a flowchart is a series of boxes linked by arrows. The direction of the arrows shows the chronological order in which activities must be completed. The shape of the boxes is also significant. Conventionally, these basic shapes are used:

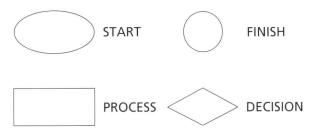

Further symbols are sometimes used to represent data, documents and other elements of the process.

Here is a very simple flowchart which shows the process a company used to handle applications for a training programme:

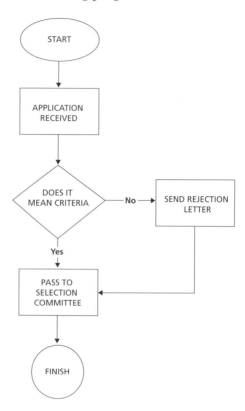

Flowcharts can help you consider whether you are really doing things in the most logical way. For example, the manager who produced the flowchart above made this comment:

'When I put the process down on paper like this, I realised that the initial screening of applications wasn't quite as simple as I had thought. It often happened that candidates misunderstood some of the questions on the form. In the past, one of our best trainees had not filled in the form correctly. If we used the system I had described on the flowchart, he would never have got on

*the training scheme. Of course, I would have liked to have redesigned the form,
but unfortunately that was something which Head Office had to deal with. In
the meantime, I was stuck with the existing version. So I added another loop
to the flowchart, like this:'*

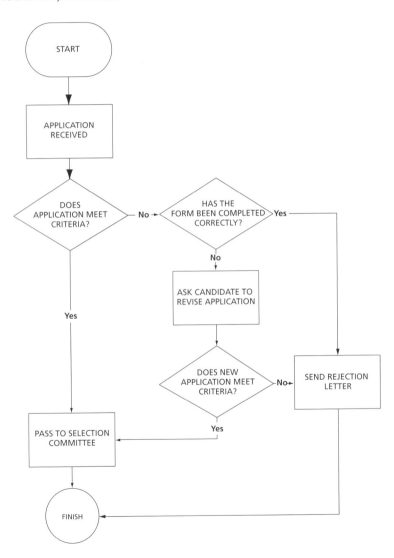

Flowcharts are also a very good way of clarifying which activities cannot begin until other activities have been completed. They can even reveal dependencies which you were not aware of:

'I drew up a flowchart to plan what we had to do to publish a new edition of one of our textbooks. My original idea was to send the old edition to a specialist editor for updating and then to ask the production department to get some costings for making up the new pages and reprinting. I quickly realised that this was not a sensible way to go about things. I had to get some costings before I invested in the new edition, to know if the project was viable. It seemed like a chicken-and-egg situation. How could I get costings if I didn't know the extent of the changes which were necessary? And how could I employ a specialist to revise the text if I didn't know whether they would make the book too expensive to market? The answer was to split the revision into two stages. First, I employed the expert to advise me on the level of changes which were necessary. Then I got the costings. Then I asked the expert to complete the job and rewrite the passages which needed updating.'

Flowcharts are useful tools when you are trying to conceptualise a project. They will highlight areas where your knowledge is inadequate or where you have not thought through all the implications of your plan. They do not, however, provide all the information you need for detailed scheduling and resource planning. In order to plan these things, you will need to draw up a work breakdown structure and, on a project of any complexity, use some form of network diagram.

Key Management Concept

Work breakdown structure

A work breakdown structure (WBS) is a method of breaking down a project into individual elements which can be scheduled and costed.

When you begin to plan a project, you are unlikely to know all the details of what has to be done. In fact, if you do have this information, you are probably not dealing with a project at all, but with a repeatable process. Projects are, by definition, unique. You cannot look back in your files and discover how long it took – or how much it cost – to achieve exactly the same outcome the last time around. However, although every project is a one-off, it is almost certain that all of the activities involved have been done before, although not in this exact combination. A WBS is a method of splitting a project up into small parts for which you can predict the resource requirements and which you can build into a schedule.

The first step in constructing a WBS is to identify the main stages of the project. These may correspond to the phases in the project life cycle:

- Initiation

- Design

- Construction

- Operation and evaluation.

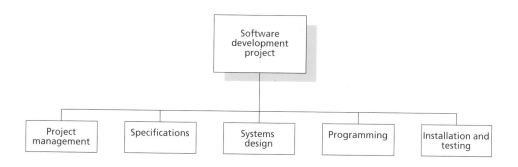

The titles – and the number – of these phases may differ, depending on the type of project and the conventions used by individual organisations. The basic structure of the project is often shown on a diagram, like this:

Once the main stages of the project have been established, the second step in developing a WBS is to divide each stage into smaller elements. There is more than one school of thought about what these elements should consist of. Some project managers simply divide the stages into chunks which relate to different areas of the project. For example, here is part of a WBS for the production of a play:

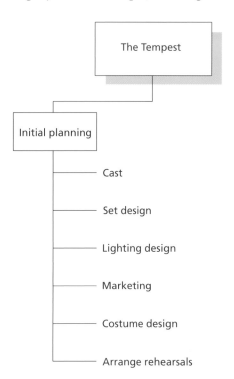

Other project managers insist that each element should relate specifically to a particular project deliverable. This approach has significant advantages, because it focuses attention on the agreed scope of the project and ensures that resources are not wasted on anything which lies outside it. It is also much easier to check that each stage in the project has actually finished.

If the elements were expressed in terms of deliverables, the example above could look like this:

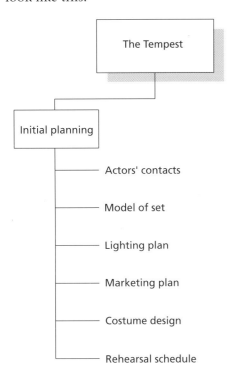

The final step is to sub-divide the items on the WBS into separate activities or tasks. On a relatively straightforward project, this may be done after the second step. On a very complex project, the WBS may need to include several more tiers before the level of individual activities is reached.

The activities listed must meet certain criteria:

1. They must be measurable in terms of cost, effort, resources and time

2. They must result in a single end product which can be checked

3. They must be the responsibility of a single individual.

We will look at these three issues in turn.

Measurable activities

The details of the resources needed to complete an activity, and what they will cost, are recorded. The total cost of the project will be the sum of the cost of all its activities. If costs change, the effect on the final costs can be calculated. The time needed to complete an activity is built into the schedule.

Key Question

How much detail do you need about the activities in your project?

It is also important that activities are on a scale that is worth measuring. For example, suppose that, at some point in your project, you had to mail 100 questionnaires to potential customers. It would be quite possible to break down the task of posting 100 questionnaires into much smaller components:

- Photocopy questionnaire

- Photocopy covering letter

- Clip letters to questionnaires

- Fold letters and questionnaires

- Fill envelopes

- Attach address labels

- Attach postage stamps

- Put through franking machine.

While it might be useful to mentally rehearse a list like this when considering what is involved in posting the questionnaires, this level of detail is not usually necessary in the WBS. As a project manager, you need to balance the control you get by specifying each part of what has to happen against the resources necessary to monitor activities in such detail. This is an area where the priorities of the project manager and the operational manager are different. If you are in charge of a busy despatch room, where hundreds of letters and packages are sent out every day, it would be important to know exactly how long it took to put 100 envelopes through the franking machine. Your staffing levels and capital costs would be calculated from information of this sort and you would need to make periodic checks that your staff were achieving the expected rate of work. However, if the posting of questionnaires only happens once or twice in the history of the project, it is not important to know exactly how long each stage in the process will take. An estimate for the entire activity will probably be enough for your purposes.

Defined outcomes

Each activity needs a specific end product. This makes it possible for everyone involved to be clear when an activity has actually been completed. It also allows the outcome to be checked against pre-determined quality standards. The aspects of an outcome which it is necessary to define will depend on the requirements of the customer, who may be either inside or outside the project team.

Here are two sets of specifications for activity outcomes. The first is for a set of briefing notes to be handed to casual staff.

The briefing notes should:

- Contain clear step-by-step instructions

- Contain a list of do's and don'ts

- Comply with company policy statement HR054

- Occupy more than two A4 pages.

And here is a specification for a press pack issued at the launch of a project:

Specification for press pack

- 500 word press release

- Three colour photographs of exterior of building

- Six colour photographs of interior of building

- Contact list for interviews

- Contents to be presented in project folder

- Copy checked by project manager

- Printed copies available by 3.7.97

The amount of detail you include in a specification will obviously depend on the importance of the outcome to the success of the project:

'We wanted to invite 50 key employers in the region to a presentation about a new training scheme we were developing. It was important that these invitations were directed at the right people within each organisation, so I specified that the PA telephoned the 50 selected companies and checked on the identity of the individual who was responsible for staff training – and also how his or her name was spelt. We also sent out a marketing shot to a much wider range of organisations. Here, we were expecting a lower percentage response and I simply specified that the PA should extract 2,000 organisations from a database which contained the names of companies with more than 25 employees. This time, the envelopes were not addressed to named individuals but to 'The Training Manager' in each organisation.'

As more importance was attached to the mailing of the invitations to the presentation than to the general mailshot, a greater amount of detail and a higher level of specification were felt to be necessary.

Responsibility for activities

Finally, each activity must be the responsibility of a particular individual. This may be the person who actually undertakes the activity, or the person who is responsible for checking that is has been successfully completed. (In many cases, these two individuals can be the same person.) Projects can involve a large team of people working together in new combinations on a wide range of activities. It is therefore essential that everything that must be done is clearly assigned to a specific individual.

Documenting the WBS

As well as the overall WBS, the project manager needs to prepare activity (or task) definition forms. A separate form is completed for each activity, giving the following information:

- Code linking the activity to the WBS

- Name of activity

- Description of deliverable/outcome

- Quality standard of deliverable/outcome

- Dependencies (description, type and who is responsible)

- Start and finish dates

- Resource needs

- Costs (amount and type)

- Individual responsible.

In most situations, a project manager will have to consult with other people, both inside and outside the project team, before describing activities in the detail required on the activity definition form. In a project of any complexity, it is not possible to know the dependencies and start and finish dates of activities before drawing up a network diagram.

Networks

Key Management Concept

A network is a diagram which shows the dependencies between the activities in a project. It is used to schedule these activities and plan the optimum use of resources.

Like flowcharts, network diagrams show the dependent relationships between activities in a project. Network diagrams also give information about the timing of each activity. This makes it possible to:

- Arrange activities so that the project can be completed in the shortest time

- Make the best use of resources

- Predict how long the whole project will take

- Construct a detailed schedule.

All networks are made up of nodes connected by arrows showing the direction of time. There are, however, two quite different types of network diagram:

- Activity on arrow (AOA)

- Activity on node (AON).

AOA networks

In an AOA network, the activity is, not surprisingly, shown on an arrow:

Event nodes at each end of the arrow mark the start and finish of the activity:

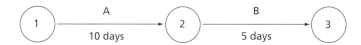

This shows that Event 1 (the start of Activity A) and Event 2 (the finish of Activity A) are separated by 10 days. The node which ends one activity can also mark the start of another activity:

This shows that Event 1 (the start of Activity A) and Event 2 (the finish of Activity A) are separated by 10 days. The node which ends one activity can also mark the start of another activity:

Using nodes and arrows like these, it is possible to construct a network which shows the dependencies between the various activities. In the example which follows, a manager describes a situation in which she needed to schedule several linked activities:

I was planning the writing and production of a technical booklet. After the text was written, it would need to be checked by experts. It would then be edited, desk top published and printed. I also needed to get a rough design done for the booklet. This had to happen before the editing stage. There were also some cartoons to be drawn sometime after the text was written and before the booklet went to DTP. It wasn't necessary for the experts to check the design or the cartoons, but the cartoons should not be commissioned until the experts had been through the text and the general design of the booklet had been settled.

The manager began by preparing a chart showing how long she expected each activity to take and the dependencies between activities:

Activity number	Description	Time (days)	Dependencies
A	write text	10	-
B	experts check	5	after A
C	design	3	after A
D	cartoons	6	after C
E	edit	3	after B and C
F	DTP	4	after D and E
G	print	5	after F

The manager then used this information to begin to draw up an AOA network:

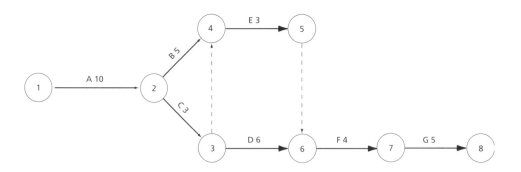

The dotted arrow between Events 3 and 4 is a dummy activity. Although a dummy activity has no duration or number, it is necessary to include it for the logic of the diagram to be correct. This one shows that Activity E cannot start until Activities B and C have both ended. (The editing and the drawing of the cartoons cannot start until the experts have checked the text and the design has been settled.) Similarly, the dummy arrow between Events 5 and 6 shows that Activity F (DTP) cannot start before Activities D (cartoons) and E (edit) have both finished.

When you draw up a network diagram, ask yourself:

Key Question

What has to happen before this activity can happen?

Now that this activity has happened, what else can happen?

At this point, the diagram shows the logical relationships between the various activities and the time that they will each take. It does not yet show the duration of the whole project or the time at which each activity must start and finish. In order to complete the diagram, more information must be added to the event nodes.

In an AOA network, each event node displays the following information:

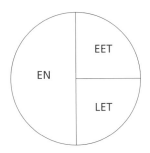

EN = Event Number: to identify the event

EET = Earliest Event Time: the earliest time at which the event can begin

LET = Latest Event Time: the latest time at which the event can begin

The diagram is completed by following these steps:

1. Start by working out the EET for each event. Begin with the node on the far left of the diagram. This is the start of the project and is conventionally given the time 00. It does not matter what unit of time is used on a network

diagram. It could be months, weeks, days, hours, or even seconds, depending on the nature of the project. It is, however, essential that the same unit is used consistently throughout the network.

2. Working towards the right of the diagram, find the EET of each event. If an event node only has a single activity arrow leading into it, it is very simple to calculate the EET of the second event. Just add the duration time of the intervening activity. If two or more activities end in the same event node, you have two (or more) EET to choose from. Take the latest time.

3. When you reach the final event node, calculate the EET as usual and then copy this figure into the LET box below it.

4. Now work backwards through the diagram, calculating the LET for each event. This time, subtract the duration of the activity. If two activities begin in the same event node, take the earliest time for the LET.

5. When you reach the first event node again, you should have a LET of 00. If you do not, you have made a mistake (either with your calculations or with the logic of your diagram) and must go back and check where you have gone wrong.

After completing these steps, the AOA diagram shown above looks like this:

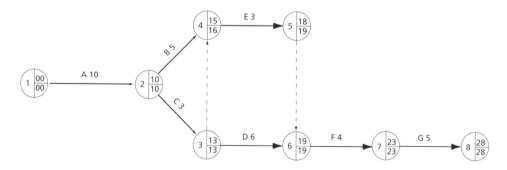

It now shows the earliest and latest time that each activity can begin or end. For some activities, there will be some extra time available. This is known as **slack**, or **float**. For other activities, the time available will be exactly the same as the time the activity will take. These are known as **critical** activities, because any delay here will delay the completion of the entire project. There is a chain of these critical activities through the diagram, known as the **critical path**. It is conventionally indicated with bolder arrows:

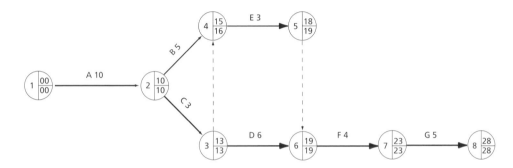

You can locate the critical path on an AOA network by identifying those activities with no float. For each activity, subtract the EET in the node where it begins from the LET in the node where it ends. This is the maximum time available for the activity to happen. Compare this figure with the duration of the activity. If these two figures are the same, the activity is critical.

Critical activities are those with no float.

Key Management Concept

AON networks

In this type of network, the details of the activities are written on the nodes themselves. The arrows are used to show the dependencies between the activities. Drawn up as an AON network, the basic framework of diagram shown earlier would look like this:

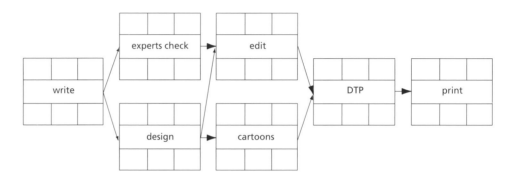

Each node in an AON network carries the following information:

Early start	Duration	Early finish
Task name		
Late start	Slack	Late finish

Once you have assembled your activities in a logical order, follow these steps to complete the network:

1. Starting at the left hand side of the diagram, fill in the earliest time an activity can start, and its duration. Use the duration to fill in the earliest time the activity can finish.

2. Move on to the next box and do the same. The earliest start time is always the same as the earliest finish time in the preceding box. If two boxes lead into one, take the later time.

3. When you have worked your way across to the node at the right of the diagram, copy the figure for the early finish time into the late finish time.

4. Now work backward through the diagram, using the durations to fill in the latest finish time and the latest start time in each box. The latest finish time is the same as the latest start time in the box connected by an arrow on the right. If you have two latest start times, take the earlier time.

5. Finally, fill in the slack time by subtracting the early finish time from the late finish time in each box. If these figures are the same, there is no slack.

The completed AON diagram looks like this:

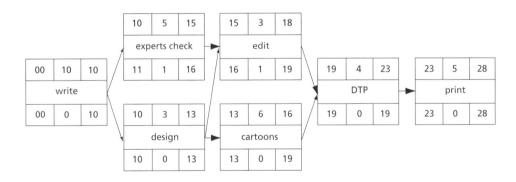

The critical path runs through the activities with no slack.

As you can see, there is no need for dummy activities in an AON network. Another advantage of the AON network is that the slack, or float, is specified on each node. Many people find this type of network easier to construct and understand than an AOA diagram.

Other types of dependency

In the diagrams we have drawn so far, we have made the assumption that an activity can begin as soon as the activity which precedes it in the network has finished. There are also other types of dependency which it may be necessary to represent on a network.

On an AON network, it is possible to add extra information to the arrow. For example, this example shows that 10 time units must elapse between the end of one activity and the start of the next:

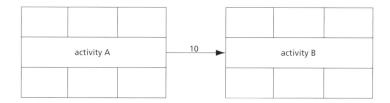

It is also possible to draw an AON network in which the arrows start, or finish, at different ends of the box, indicating finish-to-finish, start-to-start and start-to-finish dependencies.

Gantt charts

Gantt charts have been around since the 1920s. They are a simple, but remarkably effective, method of representing a project plan. They can be drawn up by hand, presented on specially designed wallcharts with magnetic or adhesive strips, or generated by a computer. The basic framework is a chart in which time is measured along the horizontal scale and activities are listed vertically.

	1	2	3	4	5	6	7	8
TASK A	▓	▓						
TASK B			▓					
TASK C				▓				
TASK D					▓	▓		
TASK E							▓	
TASK F								▓

This chart shows a simple project which is scheduled to last eight weeks. It involves six tasks (A - F) which must happen sequentially. The shaded bars indicate the duration of the tasks and the point in the schedule at which they should happen.

It is very easy to show parallel activities on a Gantt chart:

	1	2	3	4	5	6	7	8
TASK A	▓	▓	▓					
TASK B		▓	▓					
TASK C				▓				
TASK D					▓	▓		
TASK E					▓			
TASK F							▓	▓

In this chart, Tasks A and B can happen at the same time. Tasks 5 and 6 can also go on concurrently.

It is also possible to show the critical path on a Gantt chart:

	1	2	3	4	5	6	7	8
TASK A	▓	▓	▓					
TASK B		▓	▓					
TASK C				▓				
TASK D					▓	▓		
TASK E					▓			
TASK F							▓	▓

On a relatively small project, a chart of this kind can be an excellent way of showing what slack there is in a schedule. It is also possible to indicate a variety of relationships between activities. Some may happen sequentially, while others can have common, or staggered, finish or start times. These dependencies are easy to understand on a Gantt chart, especially if it is possible to move the bars which represent the activities. On a complex project, the relationships between the activities may become less easy to understand when represented in this way and it will probably be necessary to link the Gantt chart to a detailed network diagram.

In the past, the main drawback of Gantt charts was the time it took to draw them up and, even more significantly, the time it took to amend them when changes were made to the schedule. Nowadays, however, they can be generated and updated automatically by project management software programs.

Choosing your software

It is almost unthinkable these days to attempt to manage a project without the use of a computer. In this section we will briefly examine some of the options which are available and suggest some of the questions you should ask when considering the purchase of software.

The simplest type of computer programs which you may be offered for project management purposes are little more than a collection of templates to enable you draw your own Gantt charts or network diagrams. It is usually quicker to use a computer than to work by hand, and the results will certainly look more professional. However, the diagrams you produce will not necessarily be 'intelligent'. If you want to revise them at a later date, you cannot update them automatically.

In true project planning software, Gantt charts and network diagrams are linked to databases and spreadsheets. Data is usually entered into a chart and presented automatically in a graphical format. Some of these packages are extremely sophisticated. Among other features, they can offer:

- The ability to schedule thousands of activities

- What-if-analysis

- Automatic coding of activities

- Views of the project at different levels of detail

- Project organisation templates which you can adapt to the needs of your own project

- Graphs and charts showing cash flow

- To-do lists, arranged by priority

- Variance reports

- Templates for reports and other project documentation

- Pop-up help files

- Clipart to include in your presentations

- The ability to customise the design of your own charts

- Input from more than one user

- Compatibility with other software programs.

If you enjoy using a computer, you will probably find that some of the project management packages available are extremely tempting. They can give you the freedom to examine your data in a wide variety of formats and produce an integrated set of very professional-looking reports and documents. The danger, of course, is that one selects a package which is too complex for the needs of the project. However user-friendly a program claims to be, it will require a certain amount of familiarity to use it effectively. It is important to consider whether you have the time available to learn to use a program properly, or whether this time would be spent more cost-effectively on other aspects of the project. You should also consider whether the type of charts and reports it produces will be of genuine use to yourself and to other members of the team. On a simple project, a basic Gantt chart may actually be the most effective way of displaying the schedule.

Action Checklist

Here are some questions to ask when considering project planning software:

- What specification of computer does it require to run efficiently?

- What specification of monitor is necessary?

- Do I want software which will work in a Windows environment?

- Is a colour printer necessary to get the full benefit of the graphics?

- How many activities do I need to schedule?

- Do I want to use AOA or AON networks?

- Do I want to use Gantt charts?

- Do I want to be able to customise the appearance of my documents?

- Do I want the software to plan and control costs as well as schedules?

- How easy is it to update schedules and budgets?

- What types of relationship (finish-to-start, start-to-start, etc) between activities do I want to use?

- Do I want on-screen help?

- How long will it take me to learn to use this program?

- What other applications, such as word-processing programs and spreadsheets, do I want to use in combination with this program?

- Can I import data from other project planning software?

- How many people will need to use the program at once?

- What reports will I need to print out?

- What other features are important to me?

As well as looking at the publicity material produced by the manufacturers, make sure that you have the opportunity to try out the software for yourself. If possible, it is also a very good idea to talk to managers who have used the program on a similar project to your own. Ask them about their experiences. What were the best and worst features of this software? Did it ever let them down?

When you are talking to other project managers about software, it is important to bear in mind a curious phenomenon which happens to even very computer-literate individuals. Once people have spent a large amount of time working with any piece of software, whether it is a word-processing program or a project management application, they often develop a strong, and sometimes unreasonable, loyalty to it. This loyalty may make them blind to the advantages of other packages which are on the market. Bear this in mind, and do not expect to get completely unbiased advice from someone who has been using a single program for a long while.

Schedules and milestones

A schedule is a list of dates on which certain activities, or stages of the project, should be completed. It can be presented in the form of a Gantt chart, or simply as text. The following example contains a column for monitoring purposes, where the dates on which events actually happened can be recorded:

	scheduled	actual
Outline to steering group	03.10.97	
Steering group feedback	10.10.97	
D1 to steering group	17.10.97	
Steering group report on D1	23.11.97	
D2 to critical readers	27.11.97	
Critical readers report on D2	03.12.97	
D3 to pilot team	15.12.97	
Focus group	15.01.98	
D4 to steering group	30.01.98	

It is much easier to gain a quick impression of the length of time allocated to each activity when a schedule is presented on a Gantt chart. However, for monitoring purposes, a list of dates is usually more effective. It is usually a good idea to let people know the dates in the schedule which are dependent on their own deadlines. This increases their sense of urgency.

A computer-generated schedule can look impressive, but some people do not take an automatically-produced document as seriously as a more personalised, word-processed or even typewritten schedule. If you update your schedules frequently, especially if you use the same format and simply change the dates, people will soon lose respect for them. If a great deal of human thought and effort has appeared to go into the creation of a schedule, it often has more weight.

Milestones

These are significant dates in the project schedule. They occur at the end of each phase of the project and at other points, on the completion of important deliverables. They may mark the departure of certain members of the team, the beginning of a new type of activity and the time at which interim payments are made.

Milestones are usually moments for reflection and re-assessment. Like the physical milestones you pass on a road, they are points at which you can look around and consider how far you have come – and whether you are going to reach your destination if you maintain the same speed and direction. If you need to make changes to your working methods or perhaps the composition of your team, a milestone is an appropriate point at which to do it.

Milestones also have an important psychological function. On a long project, it can be extremely difficult to maintain momentum. Milestone dates provide interim deadlines, which you can encourage your team and sub-contractors to work towards. They can also provide a reason to bring a geographically distant team together to be congratulated on what has been achieved so far and remotivated for the next stage in the project.

Developing a schedule

So far, we have described how a schedule can be used to present information about the timing of activities. It is also a planning tool. The first stage in producing a schedule is to consider the constraints within which you are working. There may be certain dates which are mentioned in the contract, or dates on which events which are external to the project, but crucial to its success, occur. These dates give you your basic framework. Next, you should consider the various activities which must be completed and the dependencies which link them. The techniques of flowcharts and network diagrams, discussed earlier in the chapter, can be used to prepare a schedule. If you are using project management software, the process will probably be automated for you.

When you look at the first draft of your schedule, you may find that it uses more resources than you have available. You may discover, for example, that you have three separate, simultaneous activities which require the skills of a single member of your team. Or you may find that a particular machine is being used to complete two tasks during the same week, but is lying idle for a month beforehand.

The activities which have priority when you are allocating resources are those which lie on the critical path in a network diagram. They are the activities whose delay will cause the entire project to be delayed. Activities which have slack or float can be moved around, to level out the use of resources. Many project management programs will perform this resource levelling for you. Otherwise, the most intuitive way to visualise and carry out this process is by using a type of Gantt chart.

This diagram represents the first attempt at a schedule. The same series of tasks has to be carried out on three separate elements of a project. The bars represent the tasks, with the shading indicating three members of the team who are involved.

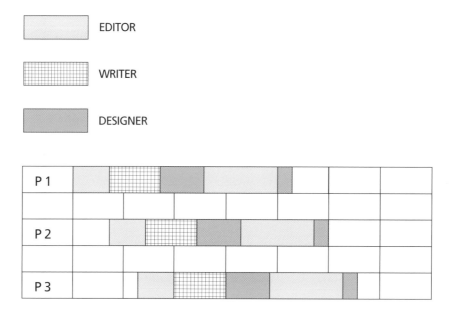

This schedule is clearly unworkable. By looking vertically down the chart, it can be seen that each individual is required to work on more than one element at the same time.

The second diagram was produced by sliding the bars along, so that no individual is engaged on more than one task at the same time. The schedule is now workable. As it does in this example, resource levelling usually involves adding time to the schedule.

Contingency

It is essential to build some contingency time into your schedule. The amount of time you allow will depend, among other things, on the complexity and risks of the activities undertaken. You do not have to tell your team or sub-contractors about the allowance you have made for slippage in the schedule. In fact, the less you say about it, the better. Extra time can be allocated for in-house processes, or activities which you undertake yourself. You can also bring forward deadlines when you present the schedule to the staff who will carry out the work.

Budgets for projects

A budget is an account of all the costs involved in a project. There are several types of cost which must be considered.

Labour costs

These are the wages, salaries and fees paid to the people who work for the project. Some of these costs will be incurred by particular project tasks and are described as direct costs. For example, if you employed an architect to draw up a plan of a building, the fee involved could be directly assigned to that task. Other labour tasks cannot be linked with particular activities. Your own salary as project manager, and the salaries of people who administer the project office, come into this category. These are known as indirect costs and are usually listed separately. If the project is taking place within an organisation, these indirect labour costs may be carried by the organisation itself and not be counted as part of the project costs. Labour costs, especially direct costs, are liable to be greatest during the implementation phase of the project.

Material costs

These are the supplies which are used up during the project. They may include anything from office stationery to roofing tiles. Material costs are usually highest during the implementation phase of a project. Most material costs can be associated directly with particular tasks and are therefore classed as direct costs.

Equipment costs

These are made up of the costs of hiring, leasing or purchasing any equipment needed for the project.

Other costs

These could include insurance, patent fees and tax.

Direct and indirect costs

The costs which can be attributed to particular tasks are known as direct costs and costs which cannot be allocated in this way are described as indirect costs, or overheads. As a general principle, greater control over costs is possible if as many as possible are linked to specific tasks, so that you know where your budget is being spent. A large burden of overheads may be inevitable, but makes it difficult to produce savings in the budget. Some, or all, of the indirect costs may be taken out of the project budget and accounted for separately. Both direct and indirect costs must, of course, be reflected in the price which the client pays.

Fixed and variable costs

All project costs, regardless of whether they are incurred for labour, materials, equipment or anything else, can be classified as either:

- Fixed costs, *or*
- Variable costs.

Fixed costs are specific amounts of money, while variable costs change, depending on the quantities involved. The purchase of a computer is a fixed cost, but the purchase of paper for the printer is a variable cost, because it will increase as further reams are bought. If a consultant charges a fee of £1,000 to provide a training session, this is a fixed cost. If the same consultant charges his time by the hour, this is a variable cost.

Fixed and variable costs can be either direct or indirect. If a building contractor buys a software program to manage a project, this would be fixed indirect cost. If he buys a central heating boiler to fit into a house he is constructing, this would be a fixed direct cost. Similarly, the weekly wage of an administrative assistant would be classed as a variable indirect cost and the weekly wage of a bricklayer would be a variable direct cost.

The problem with variable costs is that they are open-ended. They can escalate if extra materials are purchased, or the work takes longer than was scheduled. Wherever possible, project managers like to have certainty in their budgets. For this reason, a flat fee is sometimes agreed with consultants and other sub-contractors. In this way, if the work takes longer to complete, the project does not have to bear the extra cost. In other situations, it is possible to negotiate a piece rate with the sub-contractor. If neither of these solutions is appropriate, the cost must be worked out by estimating the quantity of work required and multiplying it by a unit rate. Changes in costs can then at least be predicted and explained, which gives some degree of control.

Preparing estimates

There are two approaches to preparing an estimate. The easiest way to do it is to base your figures on a similar project which took place in the past. Although this method of estimating is quick, simple and cheap, it is not likely to produce a particularly accurate forecast. If very few details are available about the forthcoming project, this approach may be the only one you can use to make a rough estimate of costs. Unfortunately, this is exactly the situation in which it is risky to make assumptions. There may be significant differences between the old and the new projects, which makes a comparison of costs completely inappropriate.

'I was once telephoned by a publisher and asked to give a quotation for editing a textbook. I had edited another book in the series two years ago, so I looked back at my records and found how much I had charged. I added a bit on to update the price, and gave the publisher a figure, which was accepted. When the manuscript arrived, I realised I had made a bad mistake. It was half as

long again as the book I had worked on previously and was very poorly written. I lost out badly on that job.'

The second approach is to break the project down into the smallest possible components, which are then priced individually. The parts are then added together to produce a total cost. This is a time-consuming procedure, but should produce the most accurate estimate possible. In construction work, estimates are prepared by costing each item on a Bill of Quantities. This document may run to many hundreds of pages and will contain exact details of every operation involved in the project.

Key Management Concept

The smaller the parts into which the project is divided for costing purposes, the more accurate the resulting estimate is likely to be, and the more expensive and time-consuming it will be to prepare.

In practice, many estimates are based on a balance between these two approaches. Some parts of the project are costed in full, while others, which are more difficult to quantify, are based on educated guesswork.

In many situations, the preparation of costs is a complex information-gathering exercise. You may have to contact sub-contractors and suppliers and ask them to submit formal quotations. Other information will come from colleagues, or other contacts, who have specialist knowledge and can advise you on the time and other resources likely to be required for the project.

You can obtain some of your data from records of previous projects. There are also various formula which you can use to calculate costs. These range from crude 'rules of thumb' to more sophisticated instruments based on a scientific study of historical data:

'When I am shooting a film documentary, I expect to shoot about six to eight minutes of film for every minute which appears in the final version.'

'Allow £x a square metre to lay a concrete floor.'

Where some types of work are concerned, formulae are available in the form of software programs and can be used to produce 'model' costings. Although they can produce accurate forecasts, they need to be used with some caution. It still takes experience of the real world to recognise whether there are any special factors which make a project untypical.

What rules of thumb do you use in your type of work? How accurate have you found them to be?

There are several phenomena which can affect the reliability of your estimates. The first of these is related to an old saying which farmers sometimes repeat:

'One lad's a lad. Two lads are half a lad and three lads are no lad at all.'

Just because you double or treble your workforce, you won't necessarily get double or treble the output. There may be other factors which come into play. Generally, the more people who share a task, the less effort each individual puts in. There are also other costs which are not scaleable. For example, you cannot usually base the cost of small quantities of supplies on the cost of large orders. Some contractors may also be prepared to accept a lower hourly or daily rate than normal in return for a long contract.

If you are calculating how long it will take people to perform a task, you need to take into account their learning curve. The first time someone does a task, they will be very slow, because they are finding out what they have to do, and the best way to go about it. The next time, they will complete the task much more quickly. The learning curve is based on the observation that, for most tasks, people improve their speed by between 80 and 90 per cent each time the number of repetitions doubles. So, if it takes one hour to do a task the first time, it will take, on average:

1 x 0.8 hours to do it the second time (0.8 hours)
1 x 0.8 x 0.8 hours to do it the fourth time (0.64 hours)
1 x 0.8 x 0.8 x 0.8 to do it the eighth time (0.51 hours)
1 x 0.8 x 0.8 x 0.8 x 0.8 to do it the sixteenth time (0.41 hours)

The more times a task is repeated, the quicker people get. The effect starts to tail off after a time, as a larger and larger number of repetitions is required to produce the same reduction in time. Ideally, you do not want to hire people for your project who have to learn how to do their jobs on your time. However, many projects do require new ways of working. For some repetitive and undemanding tasks, it may also be cheaper to hire unskilled labour and provide training than to pay a higher rate to more experienced workers.

You should also remember that people are not machines. They take a little time to reach their peak level of performance and also start to wind down at the end of the working day. If you are using standard work rates, be aware that they may be based on optimum performance, which people are very unlikely to produce 100 per cent of the time.

If you ask people to give you an estimate of how long it would take them to do a job, they may not always give you an accurate answer. There are several reasons for this. They may overestimate their capability, in order to impress you or get the work. They may overestimate how long things will take so that they can have an easier time completing the job. They may simply not know how long a job will take, but not want to reveal their ignorance. They may be naturally cautious and not want to commit themselves to a schedule they cannot keep. Your own knowledge and experience will enable you to distinguish between the estimates you should and should not take seriously, but you may still be left with a range of possibilities. In this situation, there is a useful formula which has been found to give reasonably accurate answers:

$$\text{The expected time} = \frac{A + 4M + B}{6}$$

A = optimistic time estimate
B = pessimistic time estimate
M = most likely time estimate.

Finally, when estimating costs, you should not automatically base your figures on the lowest quotations that you are given by suppliers and sub-contractors. There may be very good reasons not to accept the lowest price.

You may also need to take into account:

- Delivery

- Quality assurance

- Standard of workmanship

- Reliability

- After-sales service.

It may be worth paying a little extra to ensure that the supplies or work you are paying for really will meet your requirements.

Cost and price

It is important to make a clear mental distinction between your costings and the price which the sponsor is willing to pay. If you know that there is a budget of, say, £20,000, available to produce and print a leaflet, it is very tempting to allow this fact to influence your thinking:

'If we've got that amount of money available, we could afford to use x to do the illustrations. At any rate, we can certainly go for full colour.'

To paraphrase Parkinson's Law, it is easy to let the costs expand to fill the budget available.

It is also dangerous to try to make the budget fit an inadequate price:

'I know they will only be prepared to spend £5,000 on this job, so we'll have to cut a few corners...'

If it is impossible to do a job for the price offered, the people who are paying should be made aware of this fact. They may be prepared to increase the budget, or settle for a less ambitious outcome. On the other hand, if you go ahead with an inadequate budget, you may get into serious difficulties when the project is underway.

The project plan

At the end of the planning phase, the project manager puts together a project plan. This is based on the Terms of Reference document produced earlier, but contains much more detail on the cost, timing and specifications of the tasks to be performed. The project plan is the guidebook which will take you through the implementation phase of the project. It will need to be updated and revised as you gain more information and encounter unforeseen obstacles, but it will be a central focus of the project from this point on.

The project plan needs to be approved by the sponsor. It is often the main deliverable at the end of the planning phase. As project manager, you will keep control of the master copy of the plan. You may distribute parts of it to members of the team, or to sub-contractors, but no alterations should be made unless you authorise them yourself.

A project plan can take many forms. It may be recorded in your project software, or be presented as a loose-leaf file of documents. The project plan usually contains these elements:

The contract or Terms of Reference document

This will contain, among other things, a record of the project objectives and project deliverables and an outline of the costs, timing and specifications of the work to be done.

Work Breakdown Structure

This is a detailed WBS, drawn up to a level at which control will be exercised during the implementation phase of the project. It should give specifications for all tasks.

Costs

Estimates of all costs should be given, related to the WBS.

Schedule

Scheduled starting and finishing dates of all activities on the WBS are needed. Major milestones should also be given.

Key personnel

This section should describe the responsibilities of key members of the team. Briefing documents may be included in this section.

Risk management

This should describe the most significant risks to the project and describe the planned response. Any assumptions and constraints relevant to the management of risks should also be described here.

Management plans

This section should contain plans for dealing with specific issues, such as communication with the press, change control or payment of sub-contractors.

Other issues

This section can be used to flag up unresolved issues on which more investigation is needed or where there are decisions which have to be taken.

Additional documentation

This section may include technical specifications, designs, details of relevant legislation or standards and any other important material which will need to be referred to during the implementation phase of the project.

It is important that the project plan is organised in a way which you find easy to use. You should, for example, be able to locate key documents quickly. It should be possible to update and revise the plan and add more information, as necessary. It is also essential to impose a rigorous system of version control, so that it is impossible for out-of-date documents to be circulated.

Questions to reflect on and discuss

Activity

1. Think about the sequence of activities which have to happen when you move house. Using the planning tools described in this chapter, draw up the following to describe this process:

    *   A flowchart

    *   A WBS

    *   A network diagram

    *   A Gantt chart

    *   A schedule

    *   A budget.

    Which of these techniques did you find easiest to use?

    Which techniques were the most helpful?

2. Now try using the techniques to plan a work-based project.

Building a team

This chapter focuses on the project team. It discusses theories about how people behave in teams and how you can get the best out of the people who are working alongside you. People skills are central to project management. You need to gain and maintain the personal commitment, energy and goodwill of your team. The normal hierarchical roles which apply in many organisations are often inappropriate in the context of a project. You need to develop new ways in which people can work together.

The way in which you communicate with members of your team can have a great influence on their attitudes and behaviour. This chapter also discusses communication skills and suggests a five-point procedure you can use whenever you are planning a memo, meeting or conversation.

Many projects take place within a larger organisation. Tact and sensitivity are necessary to manage the interface between the project and the organisation. The final part of the chapter examines some of the issues you should be aware of here.

What makes a team?

Anyone who has any interest in team sports knows that a winning team is made up of individuals who excel in different areas.

'If I was selecting a fantasy cricket team, I would need strong opening batsmen to wear down the opposition. Then I would pick good stroke players for my middle order batsmen. These are the people who can put runs on, and do it in some style. I would obviously need a wicket keeper, and both fast and spin bowlers. And I would also select some all rounders, who could bat a little and bowl a little.'

In any type of team, whether it is playing for the Ashes, constructing an office block or organising a conference, different members have different functions. Another defining characteristic of a team is that the individuals within it co-operate to achieve a common goal. In a project team, this co-operation must be sustained for the life of the project and the goal must be aligned with the objectives of the project.

Key Management Concept

A project team is made up of individuals with different functional roles who share commitment to the project and co-operate with each other to achieve its objectives.

In some situations, teams arise spontaneously. In an emergency such as an accident or a natural disaster, you often find that individuals intuitively share out the tasks that have to be done and focus their energies on a common goal. Heroic deeds can be done in these circumstances. As a project manager, you need a team which will function effectively at all times, not just in a crisis. There are several things you can do to help make this happen.

Building shared commitment

You need to communicate your vision of the project to your team. It is much easier to become committed to something if you are convinced that it is really worth doing. This may involve explaining the history of the project, or the problems it was set up to solve. It may be appropriate to use some of the same presentation techniques you would use to convince potential sponsors of the value of the project. It is important that the team hears about the project from someone who can talk about it enthusiastically. If you are not a charismatic speaker yourself, you could consider inviting someone who does have this talent to address the team. Every member of your team, however humble, should be familiar with what the project has been set up to do and be able to describe its overall objectives.

A project needs a sense of identity. This may be achieved through the use of logos and headed stationery, distinctive procedures and working methods, dedicated premises and equipment, and specialised vocabulary. In a few situations, specialised clothing may even be appropriate. If people are constantly reminded that they are working on project business, they will feel like 'insiders'. However, whatever devices you use to make people feel part of the team, it is important that:

- They are appropriate to the culture of the project and the organisation in which you are working.

- They make the work of the team easier, and not more difficult.

- They are not used in situations where they could make other people feel alienated from the project.

- They are explained immediately to new members of the team.

This manager designed a special form for all internal project communications:

'I didn't want odd pieces of paper with incomplete information being passed around the project office. Whenever messages or memos had to be sent, people used a special pad. This had the project logo at the top and a space to write the date and the names of the sender and receiver. The sender had to tick one of a series of boxes to indicate the priority of the communication and note the action he or she wanted the receiver to take. It took no longer to complete this form than to scribble a message on an ordinary scrap of paper, but it improved the quality of communication considerably.'

Another manager developed special techniques for project meetings:

'Our project was based inside an organisation. We used the same meeting room that the team used for other occasions. I wanted to make the project meetings distinctive, so I re-arranged the furniture each time, setting the tables in a large square rather than a long rectangle. Instead of having a conventional minutes secretary, I got a 'scribe' to write up the action points on a flip chart as we went along.'

You should also be aware that some members of your team may not be as enthusiastic as others about adopting the 'project identity'. This does not necessarily mean that they have not committed themselves to the objectives, or that they are not prepared to work professionally. It does not even mean that they are not good team players. Some people just have their own way of working. As long as these people do not undermine the rest of the team, it is often best to allow them some flexibility. This is an area where you will have to make individual judgements.

You can increase people's commitment to a project if you demonstrate that you value their participation. Many projects begin with a meeting which is much more formal than those which follow. This can show the team that you regard its coming together as an important event. As the project progresses, you can prove that you value individual team members by not wasting their time. Do not hold unnecessary meetings or ask them to complete nonessential documentation. And try to make certain that all the equipment and other resources they need are in place for them to begin work.

Commitment to a project can also be increased if everyone involved knows what is happening at any time. There is a balance to be struck here. There may be some things which you cannot share with the team, and you should certainly not burden people with information they do not want or need, but it can be extremely motivating for the team to have a sense of the overall progress of the project. Television appeals, such as Children in Need or Red Nose Day, know that they can raise the flagging spirits of the studio audience by announcing the latest figure for the money raised. You can use different methods to achieve a similar psychological effect. Regular bulletins can remind the team of significant milestones, and congratulate the people involved when they are achieved. It can also help to record progress on a Gantt chart, or other form of easily-understandable display, in a place where all members of the team can see it.

Key Question

How will you encourage your team to share your commitment to the project?

Encouraging co-operation

The members of your team will come to the project with their own agendas. They may have:

- Volunteered because they fully support the project's objectives

- Applied to join the team because it will help their own career plans

- Been seconded to the project because there is nothing else for them to do.

They may be already committed to the project's objectives, or initially cynical about what you are trying to achieve. They may be ready to learn new ways of doing things, or be determined to carry on working in exactly the same way as they have always done. They may also have preconceived ideas about other members of the team.

Negative attitudes in the project team can lead to rivalry, lack of communication and even sabotage. Your job is to bring these people together so that they support each other in achieving the project's objectives. The first step, which has already been discussed, is to create a sense of commitment to the project. This provides a bigger context in which any interpersonal difficulties can be sorted out.

It is also very helpful to set out some ground rules before divisions arise. These may involve:

- The way in which people communicate with each other

- Working procedures

- Lines of command within the project

- Who is authorised to take particular decisions.

Make sure that team members understand and agree to these rules at an early stage in the project. Later on, if problems arise, you can refer back to them. You may have to add to these rules at a later stage in the project, but it is preferable to have the basic principles established at the beginning.

When the project is underway, make an opportunity to discuss the quality of the support that team members give each other. Useful questions include:

- What could x do to make your job easier?

- What extra resources would make it possible for you to work more effectively?

- What could the project manager do to make your job easier?

- How can we avoid a similar problem happening again?

It is important to keep these discussions tightly focused on the project objectives. Do not allow them to degenerate into personal justification or vilification of other members of the team. You must also avoid the tendency which some project teams have for excessive navel gazing. Try to establish as quickly as possible whether there are any changes in procedure which would make the project run more effectively. If there are, assess their costs and benefits and, if appropriate, set them in motion.

Finally, you can often increase co-operation if you exhibit complete fairness in all your dealings with the project team. Do not favour particular individuals above others, or insist on unnecessary restrictions. The more open and honest you can be with the team, the more they are likely to reciprocate.

Supporting different functional roles

The first thing you must do is to make sure that the people appointed to the project team really do have the skills, knowledge and experience necessary for them to fulfil their functional roles. Draw up a job specification and a person specification and make a distinction between essential and desirable attributes.

If a project is happening within an organisation, you may find that certain individuals are assigned to the team for internal political reasons. They may be there to support the viewpoint of a particular senior manager. Perhaps they are not very good at their existing job, or it could be that their current role is being phased out. Ideally, the project manager should have a large say in the selection of the project team. If this is not possible, you can avoid many difficulties by being as clear as possible about the specifications you require in your staff.

Once they are appointed, the various members of your team will have different needs. For example, they may require:

- Specialised equipment

- Particular software and hardware

- Information presented in a particular form or at a particular time

- Technical support

- Specific working conditions.

You must find out exactly what members of your team need in order to fulfil their functional roles. Although you are unlikely to be able to provide them with perfect conditions, you can at least ensure that the budget is used to enable them to work as effectively and efficiently as possible. To paraphrase the words of the song, they may not always get want they want, but you should make sure that they get what they need.

Key Question

What resources would your team like to have? What resources do they need? Can you tell the difference?

Team roles

Much has been written about the combination of personalities that make up the ideal team. You may be familiar with the list produced by Belbin (4):

- Plant
- Resource investigator
- Co-ordinator
- Shaper
- Monitor evaluator
- Teamwork
- Implementer
- Completer
- Specialist

All these character-types have their own strengths and weaknesses.

The plant

This is a creative individual who makes his or her own rules. A plant can find imaginative solutions to problems, but is impatient about working out the details. This person may be way ahead of other members of the team and can find it difficult to communicate with them. The plant needs careful handling, but can add a new dimension to the work of the project.

The resource investigator

This individual has boundless energy, especially at the beginning of a project. He or she is a good communicator and can often be the person who makes the contacts and convinces sponsors to support the project. The resource investigator tends to lose interest once things are underway and is less useful in the implementation stage of a project.

The co-ordinator

This individual is a good person to have at the centre of a project. He or she is skilled at chairing meetings and can help people clarify their goals and make sensible decisions. The main strength of the co-ordinator is in assisting other team members to work effectively.

The shaper

This is a dynamic individual who can set the pace in a project. The shaper works best when under pressure and has the drive to overcome obstacles. He or she may be insensitive, however, to the feelings of other people and can upset them with criticism. If you have a shaper on your team, you may have to keep him or her in check at times.

The monitor evaluator

This is the person who weighs up the situation slowly and comes to considered judgements. He or she has a strategic perspective and is able to make decisions which will be in the best interests of the project. As the monitor evaluator has high professional standards, he or she may be very critical of other people's work. Do not rely on the monitor evaluator for creative ideas or expect this person to inspire others. The monitor evaluator may come into conflict with the resource investigator and the shaper.

The teamworker

This individual is happy to work as a member of a team. He or she will listen to other people's opinions work constructively alongside them. The teamworker hates arguments and will do everything possible to avoid them. If you have other, more assertive personalities on your team, the teamworker can be a calming influence. This person is not a natural leader though, and can find it hard to take decisions. He or she may be influenced by other people.

The implementer

Every project needs an implementer. This is the reliable and efficient individual who actually turns ideas into reality. The implementer usually has a high degree of skill and professionalism in a particular area. He or she may be rather inflexible, however, and can be wary about adopting new ideas. The implementer is probably not as extrovert as other members of the team and may be underestimated by them. Make sure that other people appreciate the value of the implementer and do your best to convince this person of the value of the approach you are taking.

The completer

This is an extremely conscientious individual who can be relied on to do the detailed work of the project. The completer is often a worrier and will do extra work rather than trust it to anyone else. Other members of the team can be irritated by the completer's near-fanatical attention to detail. You may have to help this individual to put his or her concerns into a larger perspective. You may also have to intervene to help the completer manage his or her time and resources more effectively.

The specialist

This person has technical knowledge of a particular, rather narrow area. This knowledge is important to the project, but the project may not be particularly important to the specialist, who may only be excited by the demands of his speciality. Although you need the skills and experience of the specialist, don't expect him or her to make much contribution to the project team as a whole.

In combination, these personalities complement each others' strengths and weaknesses and can achieve great things. As project manager, you need to be aware of the areas in which your team members are weak – and also provide them with the resources and support they need to fulfil their potential in the areas where they are strong. Sometimes it may be necessary to alter the composition of the team. If your team is unbalanced by too many shapers or plants, you can provide a steadying influence by introducing further teamworkers, implementers, completers or monitor evaluators. It is often possible to bring in people with these characteristics in a supportive or administrative role. Relatively junior members of the team may have the talents you need to prevent the project going off the rails.

You may also experience the opposite scenario, in which your project team becomes too fixed in its way of thinking. Here, you may need to re-energise your team members by exposing them to the ideas of a shaper or plant. You may be able to arrange a session with one of the people who first instigated the project – or bring in an outside consultant to develop their skills or understanding in a particular area. You may need to plan events of this kind at regular intervals throughout the life of the project.

Some of the personalities described by Belbin are not natural team-players. For example, you may find it difficult to integrate the working style of a plant or a completer with that of the rest of the team. Here is how one manager handled a plant:

'The individual who had come up with the design idea for the project was quite brilliant, but absolutely impossible to work with. I would spend hours preparing papers for meetings, then he would come along and turn everything on its head. He was dismissive of the efforts made by other members of the team and upset quite a lot of people. In the end, I had to take him aside and say, 'Look, we can't go on like this. Your concept for this project is tremendous, but you are making it impossible for us to implement it. You can't put your ideas into action without the team, so please, give us some help here.' Together, we worked out some rules. We arranged to talk before the team meetings and set

the agenda. That agenda was then fixed, and he agreed not to change it. For my part, I agreed not to insist on such a rigid structure for the meetings. I also made him aware of the effect some of his off-the-cuff remarks had had on members of the team. To give him his due, he genuinely had not realised that people had been offended by what he had said. I think he was rather shocked to discover that some people were actually afraid of him. Subsequently, he made an effort to acknowledge and praise the work that other people were doing. Things did not always run smoothly, but there was much less tension at the team meetings.'

And here is the tactic that another project manager used to handle a completer:

'If I am honest, Marie was a bit of a pedant. Her attention to detail was a bonus in many ways, but it could be very irritating at meetings, where we were trying to thrash out the overall shape of an idea. I could have cut her out of the meetings altogether, but I felt that it was important that she kept in touch with the big picture. She needed to understand the concerns that other people on the project had. The solution I found was to take much firmer control of meetings. I no longer opened up a topic for general discussion, but asked people very focused questions. In the past, I would have asked, 'What do you think of John's plan?' Under my new system, I asked, 'How long would it take you to put John's plan into action?' By imposing limits on discussion like this, the meetings were much shorter and more productive. Marie was able to make positive contributions on specific points and began to have a much greater appreciation of the general pace of work and the priorities of the rest of the people involved in the project.'

Not all projects require the same mix of personalities. In a high profile project, your team should probably include several outgoing, energetic people who are excellent communicators. In a less visible project, these talents may not be so important. Some projects demand high levels of creative thought. In others, the skills of organisation and administration are more significant.

Who would be in your dream team for your present project?

Team dynamics

Teams commonly go through a succession of stages of development. These stages are known as:

- Forming
- Storming
- Norming
- Performing
- Mourning.

At each stage, the team requires different forms of support. The stages can arise over a series of weeks or months – or they can happen over the course of a few hours.

Forming

At the beginning of a project, the members of the team need to get to know each other. Some members may be unsure about what is going to be expected of them – and perhaps whether they are personally capable of fulfilling the brief. Some people may try to impose a structure or way of working that they have used in a previous project. Others may be hesitant about making any contribution until they see the way that the land lies.

As project manager, you must allow time for the group to form. Provide a structure in which people can begin to find out about each other. Do not expect to get any serious work done at this initial stage. The team will be looking to you for direction, so be prepared to give it.

This is how one project manager helped her team through the forming stage:

'I organised a weekend workshop to kick-start a project concerned with the development of a major series of training materials. I held it at an hotel in the depths of the countryside, so team members could not escape from each others' company. In the first session, I began by outlining the programme for the weekend. I then asked everyone to introduce themselves briefly. After that, I gave a 45 minute presentation, outlining the project objectives. Then we broke for coffee in the lounge. When people came back into the conference room, I could see that they had started to talk to each other.'

Action Checklist

When your team is forming:

- Maintain a high profile
- Clarify the project objectives
- Explain the ground rules
- Allow team members to get to know each other.

Storming

Many teams go through this difficult stage. People may begin to argue about the basic objectives of the project, or the way you plan to organise it. Factions can arise. People may threaten to walk out. Individuals who have not experienced this stage before may be extremely concerned that the whole project is under threat. There is often a lot of emotion around at this point. You may find that you are unable to secure agreement and co-operation on issues which you had assumed to be completely uncontroversial. You may even be verbally attacked by some members of the team.

It is essential to stay calm through this stage. Do not try to smooth over the cracks. Instead, acknowledge the conflicts, but try to express them objectively. Very often, the differences which emerge at this point appear to be much more significant than they really are. Once the issues can be separated from the emotional way in which they have been expressed, they can be examined coolly and frequently resolved. The force with which some people express their opinions at this stage often has much more to do with their own fears and suspicions than with the truth of the situation they are actually in.

This is how the project manager who organised the weekend workshop handled the storming stage:

'At the end of the first morning, we broke into three groups, representing the different functional sub-teams. The technical writers and the industry specialists had fairly uncontroversial discussions, but the training officers, who would be responsible for the development and implementation of the project materials, almost came to blows. One individual was insisting that the training programme should only be delivered by specially trained trainers. Another individual was demanding that we came up with a product that could be administered by anyone, without special training. Everyone was aligning themselves with one camp or the other. I had anticipated trouble in this area and had asked my most experienced aide to chair and scribe the meeting. When the three groups came back together, she outlined the discussion to the plenary meeting, taking great care to check that she was relaying the arguments accurately. It was much better to hear these points from a neutral spokesperson than from the protagonists themselves. They would have become too emotional and might have found themselves making statements in the plenary session which they would have regretted later. We then opened the topic up to everyone. After some input from the industry specialists, it became clear that the points of dissension were really very insignificant, and we were able to move on.'

When your team is storming:

Action Checklist

- Don't panic

- Try to anticipate difficult issues

- Allow people to express their opinions

- Examine divisions and complaints objectively

- Try to take the emotion out of the situation.

Norming

At this stage, people begin to work together much more positively. A sense of direction emerges and people start to exchange opinions and make plans. You may hear team members using the word 'we' for the first time, showing that they are identifying themselves with the project. You may find that members of the team who have been alarmed or alienated by the previous stage now feel able to make a positive contribution for the first time. It is helpful at this stage to provide definite tasks on which the team can focus. People are generally tired of arguing and want to see some positive progress made.

'After lunch on the Saturday, I split the team up again. This time we divided into four subject groups, with industry specialists, technical writers and training officers in each team. The goal was to produce an outline of the materials required in each subject area. I provided each group with a checklist of points which gave them a fairly detailed brief. At the end of the day, we came back together and compared notes. Each of the four groups had produced a viable outline. We ended the day with a real sense of progress.'

Action Checklist

When your team is norming:

*   Provide tasks on which people can focus

*   Give all team members an opportunity to contribute

*   Allow a sense of team identify to emerge.

Performing

Now things really get going. The team knows what it is trying to achieve and is working purposively towards its goal. People are co-operating with each other, exchanging ideas and finding solutions to problems. When your team reaches this stage, the best thing you can do is to let them get on with the job. Keep an eye on what is happening, but don't interfere unless you see things going off course. The team is now moving forward under its own energy and usually only needs a light touch on the wheel to steer it in the right direction.

'On the Sunday, I split the team into small groups and asked them each to draft a sample unit of the training material. Each group contained one training officer, one industry specialist and one technical writer. I gave them some specifications for the material and asked them to be ready to present their work at 4pm. Apart from that, I left it up to them. The mood was tremendous that day. I wandered around from room to room – everywhere people were completely focused on the task.'

When your team is performing:

Action Checklist

- Monitor events from a distance

- Don't interfere with the momentum of the team unless you have to

- Support the team by facilitating its efforts.

Mourning

At the end of a project, the team will cease to exist. If team members have put a lot into the project, they will probably feel a sense of loss at this point. It is important to have some kind of formal event at the end of a project, when people can evaluate what has happened and think about implications for the future.

'When the groups came back together at 4pm and presented their work, people were amazed at what had been achieved. We had the framework for the whole programme of training materials, which the technical writers could now take away and complete. The rest of the work could be done at a distance. I allowed some time for evaluation of the outcomes, and also of the process that people had gone through. Although the weekend was an unrepeatable event, I knew that some important working relationships had been forged.'

When your team is mourning:

Action Checklist

- Provide a formal end-point for the project

- Allow time for evaluation

- Recognise the value of the work that has been done.

Communicating with your team

When you are managing an ongoing operation, methods of communication can evolve slowly, over a period of months or even years. In project management, they have to be set up very quickly – and they have to work immediately.

When you make any form of communication, whether it is a quick message to a colleague or a formal presentation, you need to go through certain steps:

1. Identify your objectives

2. Identify your audience

3. Choose your method of communication

4. Match your message to your audience

5. Get feedback.

We will look at these five steps in more detail.

1. Identify your objectives

The basic question which you need to ask yourself here is:

What do I want to happen as a result of this communication?

There may be several answers to this question. You may want:

- To understand a problem

- To be able to complete a process

- To know how far a process has got

- Somebody else to be able to do something

- To convey your willingness to help

- Somebody else to accept your point of view.

Unless you are clear about your objective, it is surprisingly easy for communications to go off track:

'I telephoned the site manager and we chatted for five minutes about progress. When I put the phone down, I realised that I had not pinned him down on the reasons why we were three weeks behind schedule.'

'I dropped in on the lab unannounced to see how things were going. Everyone froze when I walked through the door. I'd intended it as a friendly visit, but the technicians interpreted my presence as a criticism.'

2. Identify your audience

You must send your communication to the appropriate person. If you don't, you cannot expect it to be successful. This may involve identifying the person who has the information you need, or the power to influence a situation you want to change.

3. Choose your method of communication

Nowadays, the project manager often has a wide range of ways of communicating with the team:

- Face-to-face

- In meetings

- By e-mail

- On the telephone

- By fax

- By voice mail

- In a videoconference

- By memo

- By letter

- By standard reports and forms

- In notices and charts displayed on the wall.

Your choice of method will depend on the speed with which you need to communicate, whether you need a written record of the communication, whether the information that will be passed is confidential, the type of feedback you need and the number of people you need to communicate with at once. For example, you cannot expect people to admit to personal difficulties with their work in a general team meeting, but you may be able to find out what is going wrong in a private meeting. If you want to make sure that all members of the team are aware of an important new procedure, it is much better to send them each a memo, rather than assume they will have read a notice you have pinned up on the wall of the project office.

4. Match your message to your audience

The members of your team will have different levels of knowledge on most topics, and different prejudices and expectations. It is important to think about how your message will be received and understood before you send it.

'I asked someone new in the office to approach sub-contractors for quotes on the parts of a job which we were not getting done by our direct labour force. I kind of assumed that he knew that the names had to be taken from the list of approved companies and that somebody had filled him in about certain difficulties we had been having with a local firm of electricians. I was wrong. He managed to approach six companies which we would never consider dealing with, including the electricians.'

You may have to send the same message in different ways to various members of your team:

'When I speak to my editors, I can be very direct about the changes that have to be made to a book. I wouldn't dream of speaking to my authors in the same way.'

You may sometimes express your message in way that can be understood by all members of the team:

'The project management software I use can produce detailed network diagrams. Of course I can understand them, but they are too complex for many members of the team. Instead, I map progress with a simple chart on the wall, using magnetic strips of different colours. Everyone can understand this.'

5. Get feedback

If you are asking a question or requesting information, you will expect a reply. If you are giving instructions or stating an opinion, it is easy to forget about receiving feedback. This is dangerous, because your message may have been misunderstood or misinterpreted. It may not even have arrived at all. You cannot know that communication has taken place unless you get feedback. When you are circulating large amounts of information to your project team, it is important to build in a method of getting feedback. And once you receive feedback, it is often necessary to alter your actions or perceptions in response to it.

We will now look at three common types of communication:

- Briefing
- Debriefing
- Meetings.

Briefing

You need to tell the members of your project team what you expect them to do. There are some instructions which it is possible to give at the start of a project, while others will have to be added during the implementation phase, in response to unfolding events. In general, only brief people about things they need to know. Too much reading matter at any stage of a project may result in information overload. If people stop reading the material you send them, they may miss vital instructions.

All written instructions should be as short and simple as you can make them. Here are some guidelines for writing clear English:

- Keep your sentences short.

- Use short words in preference to long ones.

- Write positive sentences rather than negative ones.

- Write active sentences rather than passive ones.

- Explain any acronyms and technical terminology.

- Use headings and good design to help your readers find their way around your document.

There are several devices you can use to convey instructions clearly. A step-by-step list tells people the order in which to do things:

When you receive a quotation

1. Check that the items on the quotation match the details requested.

2. Check the units used are consistent with those on the Bill of Quantities.

3. Convert items into appropriate unit costs, if necessary.

4. Check for extra conditions.

5. Enter the items on the analysis sheet.

A simple flowchart can clarify a complex decision. Here is an example of a flowchart (overleaf) which was drawn up to provide a guide to staff who were responsible for selecting software:

A guide to staff who are responsible for selecting software

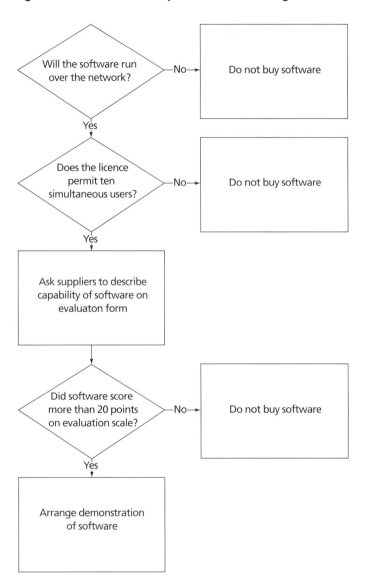

In some situations, a list of do's and don'ts may be appropriate:

DO

- Spellcheck your letters before you send them out.

- Use project stationery for all communications.

- Use first class post.

- Copy all letters to the project manager.

DON'T

- Send colour brochures out in response to telephone requests.

- Use a courier service without checking with the project manager.

The level of detail you give in your briefing instructions will depend on the experience and knowledge of the recipient. If you have put together a competent team, you shouldn't have to tell them how to do every detail of their jobs. You will, however, have to highlight the particular circumstances which apply in the project on which you are working. It is often important, either for legal reasons or perhaps to demonstrate your quality control system to your sponsors, to put certain instructions in writing.

Key Question

Take a look at the briefing documents used in your last project. Were they adequate? Could you have cut anything out? Could you have explained the process more clearly?

It is also appropriate to give some briefings orally. These can be delivered over the telephone, in one-to-one discussions and in more formal meetings. It is much easier to check that somebody has understood your instructions – and how he or she reacts to them – if you present them orally. You can also convey enthusiasm, urgency, concern (and many other things) very powerfully in speech. And some briefings have to be delivered at a particular location, where you can explain how to operate a piece of equipment or point out the potential hazards of a site. In any project, there are also likely to be some delicate issues about which you want to warn your team, but on which it is unwise to commit yourself in writing. The main disadvantage of oral briefings is that people do not have a permanent record of what was said. You can frequently avoid this problem, however, by following up with a written summary of your instructions. It is also important to consider the time that it takes to gather people together for a team briefing. You must judge whether the benefits outweigh the costs to the project.

Debriefing

You also need your team to give you information on the progress they have been making. It is up to you, as project manager, to decide the way in which this information comes to you. Many managers make use of standardised report forms which are closely linked to the project control system. If you use documents of this kind, make sure that they:

- Give you all the information you need

- Do not ask for irrelevant information

- Can be completed quickly and easily

- Can be interpreted quickly and easily

- Are directed to the appropriate person

- Are circulated at appropriate intervals.

In a project of any size, the business of gathering and interpreting information can take on a life of its own. In some situations, team members may even find that they are spending more time reporting on progress than actually making it. It is important to keep a tight focus on the information you really need. Usually, this will concern the three central issues of time, money and quality. Progress reporting is discussed in more detail in Chapter 5.

You must also distinguish between routine and non-routine information. Provide opportunities to find out about the concerns and worries of your team members, which may not appear on standardised reports.

'The weekly reports from my site manager suggested that we were well up to schedule. I would not have guessed that anything was wrong. However, when I went to see him, there was obviously something troubling him. When we were talking privately, he came out with the fact that he was very concerned about the behaviour of a key member of his team. Basically, he suspected that the man had a drugs problem.'

'I once ran a large publishing project which was administered by a team of self-employed managing editors working from home. We had a weekly reporting system. When I received the chart from one editor, I saw that he had put back the completion date on one book by eight weeks. I telephoned him immediately for an explanation and discovered that this editor had had a blazing row with one of his authors, who had resigned from the project. I should have known about this much earlier. If the editor had contacted me about it at the time, I might have been able to save the situation. Subsequently, I made it very clear to all the editors that they were to telephone me immediately if they found themselves in a situation which they couldn't handle.'

Key Question

How will you make sure that your team tells you what is really going on?

Meetings

Meetings can be a way of keeping up the momentum on a project. They are an opportunity for everyone to get up-to-date with the progress being made in other areas of the project and to remember that their own work has implications for other people. Meetings can provide a forum in which solutions to problems can be found. They can also be a tremendous waste of time.

When you arrange a meeting, consider whether there is a better way of sharing the information which will be communicated there. For example, you may be able to summarise progress in a memo, or send copies of a drawing through the post.

Meetings are often held to bring together key people to make a decision. However, the same outcome can sometimes be achieved by a series of telephone calls.

If you decide that a meeting is essential, make sure that the right people are there. On some projects, every member of the team is invited to every meeting, even though they may have no real contribution to make. Consider whether it is possible to invite some team members to part of a meeting, allowing them to get on with their work for the rest of the time.

Plan the agenda carefully. It is helpful to express each agenda point in the form of an objective. You can also direct people's attention to particular agenda items by indicating whom you expect to contribute to them.

By the end of this meeting we will have:

- Reviewed progress on prototype E4. **JG, FR, WE**

- Made an action plan for the next stage of development. **ALL**

- Decided the format for the advertising brochure. **AJ, FR**

- Agreed the print run for the brochure. **AJ, FR, PB**

- Discussed the candidates for the administrator's post and selected a short list. **ALL**

- Agreed a time for interviewing for this post. **AJ, FR**

- Discussed the implications of the report in Monday's *Daily Telegraph* and drafted a press release. **ALL**

During a meeting, somebody should make notes. It is often helpful if a 'scribe' is appointed to write these key points on a flipchart. This makes it clear to everyone when a decision has been taken. When any action is agreed, a particular individual should be given responsibility for it and a date set. These details should appear on the notes and checked at an appropriate time after the meeting.

Key Question

How useful are your team meetings? Could you make them more effective?

Working within the organisation

In the final part of this chapter we will consider the relationship between the project team and the organisation. This issue is especially important if your project takes place within the sponsoring organisation, within which the members of your team have existing roles.

Most organisations are arranged on hierarchical lines. There is a line of command from the highest to the lowest level. Everyone within the organisation knows (or at least, should know) the types of decision they can take themselves and the types of decision they must pass to the person above them in the management structure. Many organisations try to observe the principle of 'unity of command' in their structure.

Key Management Concept

The principle of unity of command states that individuals' confusion decreases and their sense of personal responsibility increases in relation to the completeness of their reporting relationship to their superior within the hierarchy.

In other words, it is much simpler and more satisfying to work for a single boss. You know what you are supposed to be doing and can take credit for the successes you achieve.

There are several ways in which an organisation can be divided up. The divisions are often made on functional lines, or by geographical area. Some companies base their structure on their product range or type of customer.

The lines of command within an organisation are often very similar to the lines of communication. People talk to their peers within their own department or unit, their immediate superior and their juniors. They may have very little contact indeed with managers in other parts of the organisation. Indeed, in many companies, there is a great deal of suspicion of the activities of other departments.

A project often cuts across the existing structure of an organisation. Individuals are seconded from different functional areas and are expected to divide their time (and their loyalty) between the project and their department. This arrangement is known as a matrix structure, in which individuals are subject to vertical (to their line manager) and horizontal (to the project manager) lines of authority and communication. It flies in the face of the principle of unity of control and runs counter to the culture of many more traditionally minded organisations. Here are some typical problems which can arise:

- The departmental manager fears that she may be losing a member of staff to the project, thus diminishing her own authority. She reacts by adding to the workload of the individual concerned, to prove his indispensability.

- The departmental manager is worried about the contacts that the project member is making with people in other parts of the organisation and withholds departmental information from him.

- The departmental manager fears that the project manager may, through his work on the project, be about to challenge her own position. She reacts by trying to undermine him.

- The project member finds it difficult to fulfil the demands put upon him.

- The project member finds his work on the project more interesting and fulfilling than his day-to-day duties, which he neglects.

- The project member may try to play one boss off against the other.

These problems can be difficult to deal with because they arise from unspoken, and sometimes unconscious, attitudes. Many of them can be avoided if individuals are seconded full-time for the duration of a project, but this is not always possible. Even if an individual temporarily relinquishes his or her departmental role, some difficulties remain. It can be awkward to move back into the department when the project is over.

The way to tackle these potential conflicts is by setting up effective channels of communication. Talk to your team's departmental managers and explain what you need from their staff. This may help to allay suspicions about the project. Estimate the amount of time that team members will spend on the project – and do your best to keep to these estimates. If you have to vary them, give adequate warning. Find out what other commitments your team members have on their time, and try to work around them. Keep lines of communication open throughout the project. Let the departmental managers know about your successes and setbacks – this will help them to see themselves as stakeholders in the project, and can greatly increase their co-operation.

Working with the culture of the organisation

The culture of an organisation shows itself in:

- The way people dress

- The way they speak to each other

- Their working methods

- The things they talk to each other about

- The methods of communication they use

- The amount of responsibility they are willing to take

- The amount of effort they put into their work.

It is very likely that the culture you develop within a project will be different from that of the organisation as a whole. Because the focus is on specific tasks, rather than on permanent structures and processes, people tend to get more involved and committed to their work. Some people who have held fairly junior positions within the organisation may find themselves working at their full potential for the first time. There is often a decrease in formality.

When people inside the organisation who are not involved in the project witness these changes, they can feel a number of different things. They may feel intrigued, suspicious or jealous. They may believe that project members are being allowed unfair privileges or that they are not maintaining the standards of the organisation as a whole. You need to be aware of these attitudes and may have to warn your project team about the dangers of antagonising other employees.

If you have managed a project within an organisation, what did the rest of the staff think about your project? Did their attitude make your work easier or more difficult?

Key Question

Questions to reflect on and discuss

1. Think about an argument or disagreement which you have experienced during a project.

    *   At what stage in the project did it happen?

    *   Who was involved?

    *   What happened?

    *   What team roles (plant, etc) were the participants adopting?

2. Using the ideas you have read about in this chapter, what could you have done to avoid or alleviate the situation?

Activity

Project in progress

Chapter 5

This chapter examines the issues which arise when a project is actually underway. At this stage, many project managers suffer from information overload. There is a danger of setting up monitoring systems which are so complex that you are unable to see the wood for the trees. Your monitoring system, however, should be your servant, not your master. When a project is in its implementation phase, your main priority should be to maintain an understanding of the overall direction of events. This chapter discusses how to set up a reporting system which will provide you with information which is relevant, adequate, current and reliable – and allow you to stay in command of the situation.

The next section of the chapter describes how quality management concepts and techniques can be used in the context of a project. In many ways, the project environment is an ideal setting for the application of these ideas.

When a project is in progress, it is important to maintain your relationship with the people who are paying for it. And, as the development of the project deliverables progresses, you also need to seek the views of the end-users. Methods of working with these, and other, stakeholders, are discussed.

All projects involve change of one kind or another, and the principles of leading people through change are described. Another characteristic which all projects seem to share is that, however efficiently they are planned, at some time or another the project manager will be faced with difficult situations. The final section of the chapter discusses some management techniques you can use to deal with problems.

Monitoring a project

The three crucial elements of a project which need to be monitored are:

- Time
- Cost
- Quality.

The project plan, which will have been drawn up at the end of the planning phase, should provide you with the framework to measure these elements. The WBS breaks the project down into activities for which you have recorded an expected finishing date, a cost and a quality specification. As each task is completed, it can be checked off, and any variance in time, cost and quality calculated.

Key Management Concept

Variance is the difference between an expected and an actual measurement.

Some variances will be within an acceptable level of tolerance. Others will be more serious and may make it necessary to change parts of the project plan. If one activity costs more than anticipated, it may be necessary to reduce costs elsewhere in the project. If an activity is taking longer than it should, this may affect the timing of activities which cannot start until it finishes. As project manager, you need to be aware which variances are significant and demand action.

Earned value analysis

This is a method of measuring how work on a project is proceeding. It involves knowing three figures for each activity:

- BCWS – the budgeted cost of work scheduled – how much you expected to have paid for the work by a particular date

- ACWP – the actual cost of work performed – how much you have actually paid for the work that has been done

- BCWP – the budgeted cost of work performed, also known as the earned value – the amount which you had expected to pay to get this amount of work done.

Using these figures, some useful calculations can be done:

Cost variance (CV)   = BCWP - ACWP
Schedule variance (SV)   = BCWP - BCWS
Cost variance index (CPI) = BCWP/ACWP

Imagine you are managing a project which involves conducting in-depth interviews with 1,000 residents of a rural area. You have scheduled these interviews to take place over a five week period. You pay your interviewers by the interview and have allowed a total of £10,000 in your budget for their wages. You are monitoring your interviewers' progress by examining the invoices they submit at the end of each week.

At the end of the first week, you receive invoices for a total of £1,500.

- **BCWS = £2,000**
  (You expected to have received invoices for £2,000 at this point.)

- **BCWP = £1,500**
  (You budgeted £1,500 for the 150 interviews which have been completed.)

- **ACWP = £1,500**
  (It has actually cost you £1,500 to get 150 interviews done.)

- **CV= BCWP - ACWP = £1,500 - £1,500 = 0**
  (Your cost variance is zero. You are paying what you expected to pay for the work. This is not surprising in this situation, since you are paying your interviewers on a piece rate. If you were paying them on a time-based rate, you could expect to see some variance here.)

- **CPI= BCWP/ACWP = £1,500 / £1,500 = 1**
  (Your cost performance index is one. This means that you are paying exactly what you expected for the work. However, if you were paying your interviewers by the hour, week or day, instead of by the interview, you would see some variance here.)

- **SV = BCWP - BCWS = £1,500 - £2,000 = - £500**
  (You have a schedule variance of - £500. This tells you that you have spent less than you expected to have spent by this point in time. It is an indication that the project is behind schedule.)

This was a very simple example, but it demonstrates that information on costs can tell you:

a. Whether you are getting the value you expected.

b. Whether your project is behind (or ahead of) schedule.

You can also do a further calculation to work out the culmulative CPI for a project.

- **Culmulative CPI (CCPI) = total of all BCWPs so far/total of all ACWPs so far**
  This gives an indication of how well you are keeping within your budget. A figure which is more than one shows that your actual costs are less than your budgeted costs. A figure which is less than one shows that your actual costs are exceeding your budget. The CCPI can give you an indication of whether you are likely to be able to complete the project within the budget – although it must be interpreted carefully. It is possible for this figure to be distorted by a particular activity which went seriously over budget and for other activities to be showing no variance. It is also possible for activities which are completed for less than their budgeted costs to mask problems elsewhere in the project.

Looking at trends

In order to gain an overview of how a project is going, it can be helpful to look for overall trends. An S curve shows figures for estimated and actual spending in a graphical form.

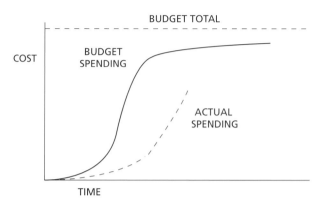

The characteristic shape of the graph is a result of low spending in the early stages of a project, before work commences, high spending during the implementation stage and a tailing off at the end of a project, when work is being checked and prepared for handover. The example above shows that actual spending is occurring later than anticipated. This indicates that work is behind schedule.

The second example shows that money is being spent more quickly than expected. This could be an indication that the project is ahead of schedule. It could also mean, however, that costs are higher than anticipated. It would be necessary to investigate this situation in more detail.

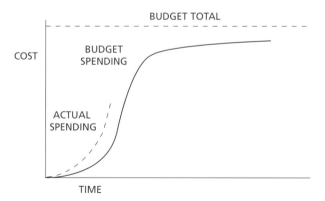

It is possible to display many different aspects of a project on graphs. With the help of project management software programs, you could produce graphs to show, among other things:

- Projected and actual cash flow

- Direct and indirect costs and spending

- Estimated and actual work rates

- Achievement of quality standard.

You can look at the overall situation, or compare and contrast different areas of the project – or even the performance of individual members of project staff. These graphs can yield important information. They can, however, also lull you into a false sense of security. As graphs produced on a software program tend to look extremely impressive, they can suggest that you are in full command of the situation, when in fact you are not. Any graph is only as accurate as the data which goes into it. If your data is based on faulty measurements or unreasonable assumptions, your graphs will reflect these deficiencies. In the next section of this chapter, when we look at progress reports, we will examine some of the problems which can arise, and what you can do to avoid them.

As well as providing an up-to-date and accurate picture of progress, the monitoring system used must also fulfil other functions. It should:

- Allow you to consider the effect of any changes in cost, time and quality on other parts of the project

- Provide a record of the project which can be used for subsequent audit.

Change control

A change in any one aspect of a project can have significant implications elsewhere. Sometimes, the people who are closely involved in the day-to-day work of a project may not be aware of these implications.

'On a publishing project, an inexperienced editor agreed a relatively small change to the text which meant that the extent of the book went up from 96

pages to 128 pages. This had a catastrophic effect on costs. She had not realised that the way the book was printed and bound meant that it was not possible to add two or three pages to the end. Pages had to added in certain multiples.'

'Because he was unable to obtain a particular raw material, one of our junior staff bought a substitute which was of an inferior grade, which resulted in more machine breakdowns. He hadn't realised that the whole success of the project was dependent on the machines being fully operative 90 per cent of the time.'

Change in any area can have implications for costs, risks, scheduling and staffing. As project manager, you may not even be aware of some of these implications yourself:

'I am very familiar with computer applications, but not with the finer details of programming. I did not realise that, by increasing the number of parameters in one calculation, I was presenting the programmers with a very much more difficult problem to solve.'

The exact implications of any change can sometimes only be appreciated with a combination of expert knowledge and an overall understanding of the interrelationships within a project.

Change control involves gathering information on any changes which occur, or are likely to occur. This information must be passed swiftly to a central control point. The project manager must then consider possible implications, discussing them with people who have specialist knowledge of particular areas. One way to gather information on the effect of changes to the project plan is to issue an Impact Analysis Form. This document is circulated to anyone who is likely to be affected by a change. It asks for the following information:

- Activities which will be affected

- Extra activities which may be necessary

- Changes to the timing of these tasks

- Other dependent tasks which will be affected

- The effect on resources and costs

- The impact on quality or specification

When a change is authorised, the project plan needs to be up-dated. Everyone who is affected by the change must also be informed. All changes to schedule, specification or cost should be communicated in a recognised format, not passed on haphazardly by word of mouth. If you are distributing revised versions of schedules, briefing papers or other project documents, it is essential to consider version control. It should be impossible for any members of the team to be working with out-of-date information.

Here are some pointers for version control:

Action Checklist

- Do not update documents more often than you have to

- Date or number each new version

- Highlight the changes you have made – or people may overlook them.

Project records

After a project is over, there are always lessons to be learned. By looking back over the details of what actually happened, similar mistakes and inefficiencies can be avoided in the future. Some records must be kept for legal reasons. In the future, you may have to prove, for example, that:

- Money was paid to certain individuals or organisations

- You took all necessary steps to maintain quality specifications.

Progress reports

In order to monitor and control a project, you need a system which will supply you with information on the progress that is being made. This information should have certain characteristics.

It needs to be:

- Relevant

- Adequate

- Current

- Reliable.

Unless you have quality information of this kind, you cannot make effective decisions. We will look at each of these characteristics in a little more detail.

Relevant information

The information you collect must be relevant. It should relate directly to the aspects of the project which you need to monitor. You will have established standards for cost, timing and quality specification in the planning stage of the project and much of the information you receive will be designed to tell you how your plans are working out in reality. As far as possible, the system you use to gather information during the implementation stage should be based on the same structure, and use the same categories, as you used at the planning stage of the project.

You should also avoid collecting irrelevant information. Do not waste time and resources gathering, processing and storing any information which will not be of use to you. It is comparatively easy these days to analyse large amounts of data, using computers. Information gives power and it is extremely tempting to try to gather as much of it as possible. You should, however, be aware of some of the dangers in this area. If people working on a project are overloaded with requests for irrelevant data, they may be distracted from the work you actually want them to do. They may be late in sending in their progress reports, or fail to complete them properly. And if you have too much information to look at, you may lose focus on the really important elements of the project. These effects can outweigh any benefits you receive from building up a large database for future analysis. Consider the cost-effectiveness of the information you receive.

Adequate information

You need to consider the level of detail that you require for decision-making purposes. Do you, for example, need staff to submit an exact itinerary with their travel expense forms, or is an estimation of their mileage sufficient? Do you need a group of people who are piloting a product to answer a specific set of questions about it, or is it enough for them to tell you their general impressions? The best way to decide what details you require is to start by considering the decisions you have to take. Think about the criteria you will use to take these decisions – and the questions you need to answer. Base your data requirements on these questions.

Current information

The information you gather should be current. It needs to be collected at appropriate intervals. The frequency of these intervals will depend on the nature of the activities involved and the degree of control you need to exercise. At the start of a project, you may need to check more frequently than you do later on, when you are confident that people know what they are doing. It is also important that the method you use to collect information allows you to see it as soon as possible. The channel of communication (post, telephone, fax, e-mail, face-to-face meetings, etc) can be important here. You should also try to avoid the necessity for lengthy compilation and analysis of data before it comes to you. With the growth of information technology, it is possible for many types of data to be recorded automatically, at the same time as a process is completed. If this is not possible, information should be recorded at the lowest level. Wherever possible, compilation and analysis should be handled by computer, so that they do not delay the arrival of the information.

An effective way of ensuring that information reaches you as soon as possible is to link the reporting system to the payment system. If subcontractors know that an interim or final invoice will not be accepted until they have delivered the information you require, you are unlikely to experience serious delays.

Reliable information

You need to be able to trust the information you receive. The individuals who provide you with data may not deliberately intend to deceive you, but they can sometimes give you misleading information. There are, however, certain things you can do to increase the reliability of the information you receive.

Ask people questions which they are able to answer. If you ask them impossible questions, they may provide you with worthless data. This is more likely to happen if you are asking people to make projections about the future.

Wherever possible, ask for information which is verifiable. Many project managers ask whether a task is 30 per cent, 50 per cent or 70 per cent completed, while others are only interested in knowing whether it is 0 per cent completed or 100 per cent completed. The second approach is safer, because a 100 per cent completed task means that there is a pre-determined deliverable which can be checked off against the schedule, budget and quality specifications.

Construct a monitoring system which has built-in checks. You may have to examine every item of data, but the people who present information to you should know that they will be caught out if they attempt deception. The system of verification should not appear as an attack on the integrity of the individuals involved, but as part of the system to ensure that the objectives of the project are met.

Encourage an atmosphere of openness and trust. If people are frightened that you will criticise them unfairly for failure, they will be unwilling to reveal any problems they are having. Instead, they will try and sort them out themselves and only come to you when they have reached a crisis. While you certainly want members of the project team to show initiative, there are often ways in which you, and the other members of the team, can support people who are experiencing difficulties. If it is tackled at an early stage, there may be a technological or organisational solution to a problem, which the person involved has not thought of. Progress meetings can be a good setting in which to discuss difficulties, but they are not always the best situation in which to bring them up in the first place. It is important that the project manager establishes a range of methods of communication, including ones in which team members can talk informally about their concerns.

Methods of reporting

You need a variety of methods of reporting on progress. Reports on the completion of tasks and on the state of the budget and schedule are usually presented in pre-set formats. The format you use for progress reports should allow direct and easy comparison between expected and actual data. With budget reports, this is usually achieved by basing the report form on the budget forecast, with extra columns for actual figures and variance. Similarly, the WBS provides the framework for task completion forms. The description of the task, the specifications of the deliverable and the individual who is responsible for seeing that these specifications are achieved, should be the same. Scheduled start and finishing dates can also be taken directly from the WBS. There needs to be space on the form to insert data on when the task actually started and finished. You may also require an explanation of any variance, and an indication of other tasks which could be affected. Any other changes, such as alterations to the specification or the process used, which could have wider implications, should also be recorded. When drawing up this part of the form, you need to be aware of the principles described above. Do not ask people questions they cannot answer or for information which you will not use.

Project team meetings are another common method of gathering progress information. These are a good method of bringing together different perspectives. If the members of the team do not see each other on a daily basis, meetings are also a good way of re-aligning and remotivating them around the project objectives. Meetings should not usually be used to report events which could just as easily be communicated on paper, by telephone or by electronic mail. However, if written reports are submitted in advance of a meeting, this can provide a useful stimulus for team members to get their records up to date and settle outstanding issues.

How much do you need to monitor?

In Chapter 4 we described the stages of development that a team usually goes through. It begins by *forming*, then goes through a turbulent period of *storming*.

In the *norming* phase, people settle down and agree working methods and relationships. In the *performing* stage, which corresponds to the implementation stage of a project, people should be working under their own steam. They should have taken ownership of the project and be working at their full potential. In an ideal situation, the project manager's role at this point should primarily be one of facilitator. Any unnecessary interference on your part is likely to distract the team or decrease their enthusiasm. You should keep your eyes on the big picture and only step in to make minor adjustments, as and when they are necessary.

Of course, you may not find that you are working in an ideal situation. There may be serious problems with particular processes or perhaps with members of the team. You may have to set up new working procedures, or new forms of monitoring, to deal with issues which you were not aware of at the start of the project. In general, the most effective approach to monitoring is to set up systems which will:

- Run smoothly and efficiently with the minimum of effort

- Enable you to see the overall implications of what is happening

- Highlight significant developments immediately

- Free up your time so that you can concentrate your efforts on areas of the project which really need your attention.

You do not have to justify your existence by the complexity of your routine monitoring system. When a project is actually underway, it is more important to direct your efforts into non-routine events. You can be much more useful as a problem-solver, a mediator and a motivator than as a time-keeper.

Building in quality

In on-going operational situations, quality management techniques are frequently used to maintain stability. Once you know the inputs and processes which are required to produce the results you desire, you stay with them, making only minor adjustments to fine-tune the system.

Techniques such as Statistical Process Control are used to calculate the limits within which processes should be performing. Control charts like the one below are developed by collecting a large amount of data and calculating what kind of variation in the process can be statistically expected. Results which lie outside these boundaries trigger a response from the person in charge of the process.

upper control line
upper warning line
centre line
lower warning line
lower control line

TIME

In a project, where resources and processes are used in new combinations to produce a unique end-product, it is not always possible to establish control limits. A process may not take place often enough for it to be worthwhile, or even practicable, to gather data which will tell you the range of results which are likely to occur. There are, however, many other ways in which the principles of quality management can be used in the context of project management.

Tolerances

In a project, specifications for each deliverable are laid down at the beginning. You know, or at least *should* know, what standards each of your deliverables should meet. It should also be possible to establish what deviation from these standards is acceptable. These tolerances may depend on:

- Legal requirements
- Contractual requirements

- Safety requirements

- Practical considerations relating to other project activities.

If these standards are measured in numerical terms – and the processes which result in these deliverables are repeated several times – a graph similar to the control chart above can be a useful tool. Unless you can draw upon historical data, the warning and control lines will not have statistical significance, but they can be drawn at points at which you judge that the process may need adjusting.

Here, for example, is a chart used to monitor the number of errors per 100 entries of operators who were entering survey results into a database:

>9									warning
9									
8									
7			■						
6									
5									
4		■							retraining required
3	■						■		
2				■				■	
1					■		■		
0									

Similar charts can be used to monitor any sensitive area of a project, such as costs, or the time taken to complete a task which is repeated several times. They allow you to identify trends and can indicate points at which you have to take action to bring the process back into line.

Quality inputs

Another important concept in quality management is the understanding that quality outputs cannot be achieved without quality inputs. This principle is directly applicable to project management. At the planning stage, quality resources should be selected. These are the raw materials, equipment, staff, information, or any other kind of resource, which are fit for the purpose for which they are intended. In a project, where you are working towards specific outcomes, you are not able to adapt your processes to suit the equipment that is available, or spend a great deal of time training staff whose services you will only require for a few weeks or months. Success often depends on being able to utilise exactly the right resources. The limited timescale and budget within which you are operating help focus your mind on your requirements.

In a project, you are likely to make short-term contracts with your suppliers. This means that you can be very specific about technical specifications, delivery, service arrangements and any other issues which are important to you. Frequently, your suppliers actually become stakeholders in the project. They understand your needs and priorities and may be able to suggest solutions to problems which you are facing. If you can develop a relationship of this kind at the planning phase of a project, it can be of immense help during the implementation stage.

Ownership

Quality can only be achieved if the people who are directly involved in performing tasks take an active interest in the effectiveness and efficiency of what they are doing. In the context of operational management, quality circles and other similar groups are set up to examine processes and look for ways of improving them. In a project, the motivation to get things right – and the organisational structure to develop creative solutions to problems – probably already exist.

The following comments are from a graphic designer working on a multimedia project:

'In my previous job, I never saw the people who used my designs. I just did what I was I told to do by the head of department and had no idea what happened to my work afterwards. I usually only did part of a job, anyway. Somebody would ask me to design a series of buttons or a title screen, and I was not really aware of the whole context. When I worked on a small project, things were very different.

'I was part of a team which consisted of a programmer, a subject expert and a writer. At our first meeting, I was waiting for them to tell me what to do,

then I realised that they were expecting me to come up with some ideas. It was the first time since I had completed my training that I had so much responsibility for the end-product.

'*The opportunity to work with other specialists was a real eye-opener. Often, in meetings, I would suggest things, and the programmer would say, 'Yes, that's not a bad idea, but it would work better if you could use the same range of colours as you used in the other part of the screen, then the computer won't have to handle two palettes at the same time.' Or the subject expert would say, 'Your text is too small there. Those are the points which people find really difficult to understand – you need to give them much more prominence.' And sometimes the advice went in the other direction, too. I was able to suggest to the writer that we could dispense with a complicated numbering system and use colour to identify different parts of the text.*

'*I no longer felt that I was just doing a nine-to-five job. As the project progressed, it really mattered to me that the final product was as good as it possibly could be. I knew that my name would be on the credits, and I wanted it to be something I was going to be proud of.*'

In any sector, people who habitually work on projects know that they are 'only as good as the last job they worked on'. Reputations are built and lost on projects, where the final product is closely identified with the team which brought it about. There is a strong incentive for people to commit themselves fully to a project and perform at a high level.

The limited time scale of a project can also increase a sense of ownership and commitment. People can become very involved with something which they know is only going to last a few months, although they would not be prepared to put in the same amount of effort on a permanent basis. For these reasons, many companies try to organise an increasing number of their activities on a project basis.

Customers and suppliers

Quality management is based on a chain of customers and suppliers, which may be either external or internal to the organisation. At each interface, customers and suppliers identify and discuss their requirements. We have already seen how the need to specify inputs, and the contractual arrangements with suppliers, highlight this relationship. There are also other customer-supplier relationships within a project.

The project manager is a supplier to the client or sponsor, whose requirements are clearly defined in the Terms of Reference. Everything which happens in a project is designed to meet these requirements. If changes to the scope, cost or timescale are necessary, these must be negotiated and agreed.

In the implementation stage of a project, the project manager is actually a supplier to the project team. You must provide them with the equipment, raw materials, guidance, working conditions and technical support they need in order to do their work. And the members of the team are also your suppliers. They must deliver work at the cost and time and to the specification which you have set. Because of the dependencies between the various activities which make up a project, individual members of the team also have customer-supplier relationships with each other. A project cannot succeed unless those involved in its various activities are aware of each others' requirements and do their best to meet them, even if this means taking a new and more flexible approach to their own work.

Key Question

In the last project you worked on, who were your customers? And who were your suppliers? How did you have to adapt yourself to their requirements?

Quality outputs

Within a project, definite standards are set for each internal deliverable. It is the project manager's responsibility to ensure that these standards are set out clearly, so that everyone involved knows exactly what they are supposed to be achieving. When people are working on a contractual basis, payment can be linked to the most important of these deliverables.

It is also necessary to consider the final outcome of the project. If you are working on a new product or service, this will need to be tested on the end-user. In a large project, the reactions of customers will probably be investigated by specialist market researchers. There are some general points, however, which it is useful to remember in other situations.

If you are asking end-users what they think, be prepared to listen to what they tell you. If the feedback you receive is unfavourable, it is very easy to dismiss it as uninformed or irrelevant. The greater your own commitment to a project, the more difficult it can be to accept criticism from outside. For this reason, it is often better for pilots to be conducted by individuals who can put some distance between themselves and the project.

Get the timing right. Do not leave piloting until the last moment, when it will be extremely difficult to make changes to the design or specifications of the product or service. Contact with end-users should be built into a project from the very beginning, so that the original objectives and scope are informed by their opinions. It is often important to talk to end-users, or at least of experts who are familiar with their requirements, throughout the life of a project.

If you are presenting an unfinished product, make this clear. People who are unfamiliar with the development process may expect to see something which corresponds to commercially available products or services and may reject what you are showing them because it does not conform to their experience. If it is possible to do so, it may be advisable to take one example of your product to a finished form.

Ask appropriate questions. Guide the end-user to the areas where you want information. Adapt your terminology to your audience. For example, if you wanted to investigate the effectiveness of the design of a leaflet, your questions might include:

- What pictures can you remember seeing in the leaflet?

- How easy was it to find the information you needed?

In a questionnaire or a formal interview, closed questions, which offer respondents a limited range of options, are often used. The answers to these questions are easy to analyse, but the type of information that you receive is limited by the options you provide. Open questions, where respondents are free to answer in any way they want, can reveal more. They are much more difficult to analyse, however, and also need to be carefully presented. If people are faced with a series of open questions, they may not know what type or level of answer you expect them to give, and fail to respond or only give perfunctory replies. You may only receive full replies from people who feel very strongly about the product, which may distort your results.

Some people may also be unwilling to tell you what they really think. If they have been invited to try out a product or service, they may feel constrained to be polite. Others may be over-critical. There may also be other reasons why people will not reveal their true reactions. Many interviewers use projected questions to get around this difficulty:

- How frequently would you say that most people use a personal deodorant?

- Would a price of £200 be about right, or too much for many people to consider?

- Do you think that parents take enough interest in what their children watch on television?

People are sometimes much more forthcoming about what others think, do or believe than about their own behaviour and views.

Working with stakeholders

It is important to maintain your relationship with the sponsoring organisation while the project is in progress. After the initial negotiations are over and contracts are signed, contact between the project and the organisation which is paying for it will probably be directed through a single member of staff. This individual can be your spokesperson and champion within the sponsoring organisation. If things go badly, he or she can also be instrumental in withdrawing sponsorship from the project.

Consider the needs of this individual. Apart from the progress reports and other forms of documentation described in the Terms of Reference, the representative of the sponsoring organisation may also be looking for:

- Personal insight into the work of the project

- Examples of what is happening which can be shown to other managers

- Advance warning of any difficulties which may arise

- Confidence that any assurances that he or she makes on behalf of the project will be honoured.

Once contracts are signed, the sponsor should be your ally, not your adversary. You are, after all, committed to the same objectives.

Key Question

What actions can you take to encourage a relationship with your sponsor of trust and mutual respect?

Other stakeholders

You can also do a great deal to foster good relationships with other stakeholders. The people who are working directly for the project are likely to be influenced by the following factors:

- Rate and speed of payment

- Acknowledgement of the contributions they make

- Clear guidance

- Support when it is needed.

Here are some comments on good and bad experiences from people who have worked on projects:

'I came up with rather an ingenious solution to a technical problem. It wasn't an earth-shattering development, but it was a neat piece of design. I must say that I was rather flattered when the project manager described what I had done at the team meeting. It's nice to be appreciated.'

'I pulled out all the stops to meet my deadline. I scarcely spoke to my family for a couple of weeks and put all my other work on hold. I was pleased to do it, because I knew that other people in the team were depending on me. However, when I submitted my invoice it languished on somebody's desk for a couple of months before it was finally paid. I was financially inconvenienced by this delay, and I also felt cheated, as though I had been taken advantage of. It left an unpleasant taste in my mouth, somehow.'

'The most irritating project manager I ever worked for had this habit of saying 'Yes, tremendous, fantastic work!' when you showed him what you had been doing. Then he would come back a couple of hours later, or perhaps the next morning, and say, 'Look, I've been thinking. Perhaps there are one or two changes we ought to make...' I hate working for someone who doesn't know his own mind.'

'I was let down by a sub-contractor and telephoned the project manager to discuss the problem. Instead of blaming me for getting into the situation, she was completely practical in her approach. Together, we worked out a rescue plan. She provided me with all the resources I needed and, as I later discovered, took responsibility for the incident on her own shoulders. That is what I call support.'

In some projects, your stakeholders will include local residents. It is often good public relations to supply the local press with stories about current developments. This will increase anticipation for the final product or service and can help diffuse annoyance about any inconvenience you are causing them. In other situations, your 'public' may be an industrial sector or perhaps an academic community. Here too, interim reports in the specialist press can provide good pre-publicity. It is absolutely essential, however, that any information which you release about the project is agreed with the sponsoring organisation. They probably have their own plans for publicity.

Earlier in this section, we discussed the importance of consulting end-users. As well as helping you to develop the product, these contacts can also bring other benefits. By issuing a trial version of a new product at a very attractive price, it is sometimes possible to conduct a mass pilot and simultaneously develop a market. If customers feel they have played a part in developing a product, they may feel a sense of loyalty to it later.

Leading people through change

All projects involve change of some kind. This change may be trivial, or it may have a profound effect on people's lives. Many of your stakeholders may be apprehensive about the consequences of your project and oppose it in any way they can. An understanding of the principles of change management can help you avoid some of this opposition.

Force field analysis is a technique which was developed by Kurt Lewin, a social scientist. It is based on the theory that people and organisations act in the way they do because of the combined effect of opposing forces. Some of these forces propel them in one direction, while others push them in the opposite direction.

The result is a state of equilibrium, in which the both sets of forces are exactly balanced.

The forces which keep the situation in equilibrium can include:

- What people believe

- What people understand

- What people fear

- Costs

- Benefits

- The resources that people have available to them.

As long these forces remain in equilibrium, the situation will not change. If you want to change the situation, three steps are necessary:

1. Destabilise the existing equilibrium

2. Move to a new position

3. Stabilise the new equilibrium.

The current equilibrium can be destabilised by introducing a new driving or restraining force, or by strengthening or weakening any or all of the existing forces. For example, if you wanted to persuade people to accept a change in their working methods, you would start by considering what forces were operating to maintain the present equilibrium:

'I was engaged on a project to develop and implement a new information system within an organisation. I wanted to change the current habit that staff had of putting most internal communications on memos and encourage them to use e-mail instead. I began by talking to staff and considering the driving and restraining forces which maintained the status quo. It seemed to me that the most significant reason why people used memos was:

- *They wanted to stay in frequent contact with other members of staff.*

The main restraining forces, the reasons why they didn't want to move to another system, were:

- *They were unsure how to use e-mail*

- *They felt worried without a written record of their internal communications*

- *They were uncertain about the security of e-mail.*

I saw that the driving force in this situation, the desire for frequent communication, could equally well apply to e-mail. The issues I had to concentrate on were the restraining forces. I decided to remove people's lack of confidence and worries about insecurity by addressing these points in training sessions. The worry about a lack of written records was slightly more difficult. I didn't want to encourage them to print out all their messages for the paper-based filing system. In the end, I decided that the best way forward was to educate them in the use of electronic filing systems. I showed them how, with the use of directories, sub-directories and simple codes, they could have much more efficient access to their documents.'

When people are faced with a change, they commonly go through the following stages:

- Shock

- Opposition

- Exploration

- Acceptance.

Shock

In the initial stage, when the change is first announced, it is important to give information clearly and simply and allow a little time for it to be absorbed. People's initial reaction may be very emotional, especially if they believe that the change is an adverse one. It is important to stay calm and not respond in kind to any emotional outbursts.

Opposition

Once people have collected themselves, they are likely to respond with opposing arguments. These may reflect a desire to keep things as they are. Other people may respond with apathy, cynicism, withdrawal from the debate or anxiety. Self-appointed 'leaders of the opposition' may arise and factions may form, causing internal divisions. Allow people to voice their reactions and treat these views with respect. Provide as much information as you can to avoid the development of rumours. Keep communications as open as possible, so that everyone feels involved.

Exploration

In the third stage, people begin to consider how the changes will affect them. They want to understand the full implications of what is going to happen. People may still be confused, but they are beginning to realise that the change is inevitable. Slowly, they will begin to feel more positive about the future. You can encourage this new mood by involving the people concerned in working out the details of the change.

Acceptance

In the final stage, the change process is almost over. At this point, you should check that the anxieties expressed earlier in the process have been allayed and that any undertakings made while the changes were under discussion have been honoured. This will make people more willing to trust you when you have to introduce another change.

Dealing with problems

However carefully you have laid your plans, it is extremely likely that events will not turn out exactly as you had imagined. A key member of your project team may fall ill, or not be quite as skilled as you had thought. Suppliers may let you down with late deliveries. Equipment may fail. New legislation may mean that you have to revise your specifications or working methods. As the activities of the project become more visible, you may run into opposition from groups or individuals. And the more complex a project is, the more things there are which can go wrong. As a project manager, you must be able to deal with the unexpected. In this section we will examine some of the techniques you can employ to get a project back on track.

Dealing with difficult people

In Chapter 4 we looked at the character stereotypes which combine to make the project team. All these personalities have their strengths, but they also have their weaknesses. We also discussed some tactics you can use to deal with personality clashes, or situations where one individual is holding up the work of the project.

Sometimes, you may have to take drastic action. If a member of the team proves to be totally inadequate, you will probably have to dispense with his or her services. If you have to do this, it is best to recognise the fact as soon as possible and do the deed quickly, before the morale or performance of other people is affected. However, there may be repercussions. The departure of a team member can breed fear and distrust in those that remain. If people feel vulnerable, they may not be quite as eager to come to you with their difficulties. You will also have to find and train up a replacement. Until the replacement is in place, the rest of the team may experience hold-ups or have to do extra work.

Sometimes you can solve the problem by changing people's roles. It is important to do this in a way that does not appear to be a judgement on their own shortcomings. You should focus on the needs of the project, not on personalities. If you introduce new rules, make them apply to everyone, not just the individual who is causing you problems. If you are really skilled, you can convince the person involved that the changes you require in their behaviour or working practices are their own idea:

> **Project manager:** *John, I wonder if we could have a quick word before the others arrive. I'm getting a bit concerned about the time it is taking to process purchase orders. Once or twice I have telephoned a supplier to query a late delivery and they have said that they have only just received the order, when I would have expected them to have received it at least a week ago. I was wondering if you could suggest any way in which we could speed the procedure up. Just take me through what happens, could you?*

> **Administrator:** *Well, the purchase order arrives on my desk and I check it against the budget, and then I get the relevant budget holder to sign it, and then I send it to the supplier, with a copy to accounts.*

> **Project manager:** *And how many requests do you get a week, on average?*

> **Administrator:** *It could be 40 or 50.*

Project manager: *That's a lot. But they are not always for large amounts?*

Administrator: *Oh no, most of them are for less than £20. Some are under £10.*

Project manager: *It seems that a lot of effort is necessary on your part to deal with relatively small amounts of money. And it can't always be easy to find a budget holder at short notice.*

Administrator: *Well, that's the problem. I can't always find someone to sign the order.*

Project manager: *And we really should be getting the orders processed within two working days. I wonder if we are right to use the same procedure for all orders.*

Administrator: *We could... Well, how about if I was able to sign orders myself, up to a ceiling of, say, £20?*

Project manager: *That's not a bad idea. But I'm still a bit worried about the amount of paperwork you've got on your plate.*

Administrator: *Well, how about if core team members could sign orders themselves, up to £20, and then they were to pass a copy to me, so I could keep the records up-to-date and check that no-one was misusing the system?*

Project manager: *That sounds like a very good suggestion. I'll delegate part of the budget to core team members and draw up some guidelines, so they understand the limits we are working within. And, of course, you will continue to deal with all the important orders in the traditional way. If we set this system up, your desk should be a lot clearer, so what turnaround time do you think you could achieve with the orders over £20?*

Administrator: *Oh, two working days. No problem.*

Project manager: *Excellent. That should speed things up a lot. I'll send a memo round saying that all purchase orders must be sent out within* *two working days of the original request for supplies being made. Let's have another chat in a couple of weeks and see how the new system is working.*

The project manager handled this situation with great tact. You may not always have the need – or the opportunity – to be quite as sensitive as this. However, if you want to retain the loyalty and enthusiasm of your team, it is as well to avoid upsetting them unnecessarily.

If you need to change the way someone is working:

- Focus on the project, not personalities
- Don't criticise their work in front of other people
- If possible, get the person involved to suggest a solution
- Ratify the solution with your own authority
- Apply new procedures to everyone
- Check that the solution has solved the problem.

Problem solving

It can sometimes be hard to think straight when you are under pressure. If a problem arises, it is tempting to make a snap decision and implement the first solution which comes to mind. However, whenever possible, it is well worth taking the time to go through a simple procedure:

1. Define the **boundarie**s of the problem
2. Identify the **cause** of the problem
3. Devise a **range of solutions** to deal with the problem
4. Select the **most appropriate** solution.

Instead of reacting instantaneously when something goes wrong, consider how big the problem really is.

Ask questions like these:

- How long has this been going on?

- How wrong were we in our estimates?

- How much is it costing us?

- Who is involved?

- Does it happen all the time?

This will enable you to see how serious the problem is – and which activities or personnel are (and are not) involved.

'I had an angry telephone call from a resident who lived opposite the site where we were working. He said that our vehicles were always blocking the road, making it impossible for people to get to work and he had contacted the police. I phoned the site manager and established that there had been a problem that morning, when a delivery lorry had been trying to back through the gates and had held up the traffic for 20 minutes. He was expecting further similar deliveries over the next few weeks.'

Next, look for the causes of the problem. A useful technique to use here is to ask yourself a succession of 'why?' questions:

- Why did the lorry block the road?
  Because it had to back into the gates.

- Why?
  Because it was too big to turn round in the yard.

- Why?
  Because the suppliers sent a big lorry.

- Why?
  Because it's the only one they've got.

This series of questions can often suggest a solution. In this situation, it may be possible to use a different supplier who has a smaller lorry. Other solutions may be possible, too:

- Arrange for supplies to be collected from the supplier

- Ask the supplier to delivery at another time of day, when people are not trying to get to work

- Use another entrance

- Next time you are expecting a delivery, warn the residents the evening before, so they can move their cars to the end of the street.

Finally, when you have assembled a range of options, choose the most appropriate solution:

'I telephoned the manager of the suppliers, explained our problem and asked him to make sure that future deliveries were scheduled for the middle of the day, when local people were less likely to be using the road.'

This was a simple problem to solve. Sometimes, you may be faced with a situation where the causes are much more difficult to identify. In this case, it may be helpful to use an Ishikawa or 'fishbone' diagram. Start by writing the effect in a box, with an arrow pointing to it. Then think of a few categories which the causes might fall into. Common categories are:

- People

- Processes

- Materials

- Equipment.

Set up arrows for each of your categories. Then think of possible causes within each category and write them on the diagram. The fishbone diagram is a good way of analysing a problem. It can help you to think of causes which might not have occurred to you immediately.

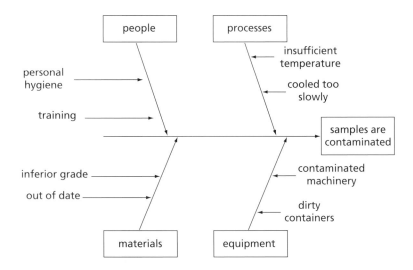

Problems with the schedule

In project management, there are some established methods of solving problems with the schedule.

Bringing in extra resources

If the work is taking longer than anticipated, it is worth considering increasing the resources deployed on the project. This may involve bringing in more staff on a temporary basis, paying staff to work longer hours, sub-contracting tasks or using more expensive equipment. A mathematical trade-off is made between the cost of falling behind schedule and the cost of increasing resources. If you assign work to inexperienced individuals, you will probably suffer some loss of efficiency while they learn what is expected of them. If you use people who are already proficient at the task, you may have to pay a great deal for their services, especially if you find them through an outside agency. This latter option, however, is often the best alternative.

Fast tracking

Instead of waiting for a task to be completed before starting the task which depends on it, you can sometimes split the first task into sections and start the dependent task before the first one has finished. On paper, the time savings can look impressive:

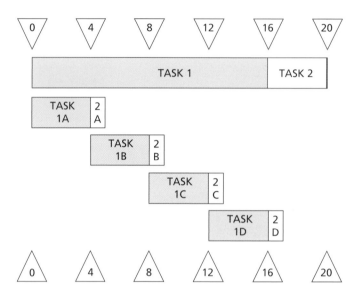

Before fast tracking, tasks 1 and 2 were scheduled to take a total of 20 days. After fast tracking, with task 2 starting before task 1 ends, the scheduled time is cut to 17 days. The savings arise because work is being done on both tasks simultaneously.

The problem with fast tracking is that some of the early work may have to be redone, as issues which affect the whole of the first or second task may not emerge until the whole of the first task has been completed.

'To save time on a schedule, I arranged for the statistical analysis of some research results to begin as soon as we had inputted the first batch of data from our questionnaires. Unfortunately, when the third batch of data was put on the computer, I realised that we needed to revise the categories we were using for the analysis. The work on the first and second batches of data was useless and had to be done all over again.'

Questions to reflect on and discuss

1.   Draft a collection of monitoring documents to be used in a small-scale project.

2.   Will they provide you with information which is:

    •   Relevant?

    •   Adequate?

    •   Current?

    •   Reliable?

Activity

The end of the story

Chapter 6

This is a very short chapter. It describes what happens at the end of a project, when you present the results of your efforts to the people who commissioned the project. The way in which you do this can have a significant effect on the reception which the final deliverables receive. The chapter outlines the administrative details which have to be taken care of when a project comes to a close. It also provides a list of questions you can ask yourself about how the project went, in order to learn lessons for the future.

In the last section of the chapter, attention turns back to the project team. One of your final responsibilities as project manager is to do your best to ensure that the project ends well for the people who have contributed to its success.

Delivering the goods

A project reaches its climax when the final and most important deliverable is presented to the client. Even though you will have been in close and continuing communication with the organisation which has paid for the project, this is the moment of truth.

If you have kept your client properly informed of developments throughout the project, there should be no big surprises at this point. It cannot be denied, however, that there is something different about seeing the completed version.

'I had been closely involved in a documentary video which my company was sponsoring. I had visited the location during filming, helped select the music, seen the first assembly, made some alterations to the commentary and approved the final version. But when I went into the viewing theatre and sat in a proper cinema seat, and the opening credits began to roll, I must admit that the hair on the back of my neck stood up. It was as though I was watching the video for the very first time.'

When clients are about to receive the final outcome of the project, they are usually slightly anxious. Will they get what they expected? Have they got value for money? You can help alleviate this anxiety by making a good first impression.

Think about small details of presentation. For example, if you are handing over a renovated building to a client, the floor should be clean and all building materials be cleared away. If you are handing over a set of training manuals, they should be attractively bound. If you are presenting a CD containing a computer program, check that the machine on which you will show it is configured properly, so that the colours are not distorted.

You should also make sure that adequate explanations are provided. In some circumstances, a member of the project team may talk the client through whatever is being presented. If you take on this explanation yourself, it is often advisable to have a technical expert from the team on hand, to deal with any difficult questions. In other situations, full documentation may provide the necessary explanations. As soon as possible after the presentation, let the clients experience the deliverable for themselves. Encourage them to pick it up, glance through it, walk round it – or do whatever is necessary to take possession of it.

Project closure

At the end of a project, there are administrative procedures to be attended to. The results of the project need to be checked and documented, often in the form of a final report to the client. This report may contain an evaluation of the project's processes and outcomes.

Final payments to sub-contractors and others have to be made. There may be equipment or surplus supplies to dispose of and leasing agreements to bring to a close. All project documents and databases should be brought up to date and compiled into an archive. The documents that are kept will probably include:

- All financial records, including invoices, receipts and purchase orders

- Contracts

- Letters and other internal and external communications

- Minutes of meetings

- The project plan, in all its versions.

On a project of any size, an extremely large collection of documents will need to be archived. It is essential that these papers are properly catalogued, so that it possible to find individual items in the future. If any legal or contractual aspect of the project is questioned at a later date, the archive can provide evidence of what actually happened.

Part, or all, of the contents of the archive may be required by the client or sponsor for their own records. It is also important that the project manager keeps copies of some documents. You may need them if you are challenged about any decisions which you have taken. You will also need them to complete your own evaluation of the project and as a source of historical information to be drawn on when you embark upon your next project.

Evaluation

When a project is over, there are many lessons to be learned. The client is usually most interested in evaluating the outcome, which will be measured against the original objectives. The client will also want to know whether the objectives were achieved within the budget and schedule – and to the right specifications. If any of these elements changed in the course of the project, full explanations must be provided. In addition, the client will want to know whether the assumptions made at the start of the project proved to be correct and which, if any, of the risks materialised. All this information will be helpful when the next project is commissioned.

The client will also take a wider view of the project. When the outcome is finally in the hands of the end-users, their reactions will be sought. Even if a project has gone exactly to plan, with all deliverables produced to specification, it can still be a failure if the customers do not like the outcome. If this happens, the basic concept behind the project may have been wrong. It is not usually advisable to complete an evaluation of this sort until the results of the project have had time to settle down and can be looked at in a broader context.

The project manager has a different perspective on evaluation. Your own focus is likely to be on processes, rather than outcomes. You need to learn any lessons you can which will increase your effectiveness and efficiency in future projects. Here are some useful questions to ask:

- What changes were made to the project plan and why were they made?

- What were the strengths and weaknesses of the staff, suppliers and sub-contractors used?

- How effectively were communications managed?

- What planning tools were used and how effective were they?

- What aspects of the project could have gone better?

- How effective were the monitoring and control systems?

- How accurately were resource needs estimated?

- Is there any data about resource use which I can make use of on a future occasion?

- What mistakes were made and how could I avoid them happening again?

- What would I do differently if I was embarking on the project with the benefit of hindsight?

Some of these questions can be answered by looking through the records which have been kept from the project. Others can only be answered after personal reflection.

Saying goodbye

In the final section of this chapter, we turn our attention back to the project team. This group of people has worked with you throughout the preceding weeks or months, and now has to be disbanded. Towards the end of a project, the team often diminishes in size. As individuals complete the activities for which they are responsible, they may start on new contracts elsewhere or be re-assigned to other work within the organisation. At the end of a project, the central core of the team is often all that remains. You may even be working in isolation.

At some stage, either before or after the delivery of the final project outcome, it is important to bring the team together again. If people have drifted away from the project over a period of time, they may be left with a sense of anticlimax or a feeling that something has been left unfinished. A formalised occasion is necessary to mark the end of the project.

These two accounts describe the effect that such an occasion can have:

'When the arts centre I had worked on was finished, everyone who had been involved was invited to bring their families to a special open day. I rarely get the chance to show my wife and children my work, so this meant a great deal to me.'

'The last weeks of the project had been a nightmare, beset with problems. We had driven ourselves so hard to achieve our deadlines. At the end I said 'Never again!' And then I went along to the final project meeting. The project manager had organised a buffet lunch and bought a small gift for each member of the team – nothing expensive, just a paper knife inscribed with the name of the project. I must admit that I was rather moved. Suddenly I was able to remember the good times as well as the bad times and was extraordinarily proud of what we had managed to achieve. I've kept the paper knife. In fact, it's in front of me, on my desk, now. It's a nice reminder.'

People can get emotionally affected at the end of a project. The greater their involvement and commitment, the greater their reaction is likely to be when it is all over. You could not have completed the project without the support of your team, and it is right to congratulate and thank them at the end. This is not sentimentality, but a decent acknowledgement of the contribution they have made.

A good finish to a project can help people to forget many of the problems they encountered along the way. It will increase their self respect – and also their respect for you as a project manager. It may also make them eager to work with you again in the future.

Questions to reflect on and discuss

1. Think about a project you worked on in the past.

    Complete the following sentence in as many ways as you can:

    If only I had known... at the beginning, I would have...

2. What steps will you take to ensure that you DO have this kind of information on the next project that you manage?

Activity

Bibliography

Chapter 1

1. Olsen, R P, *Project Management Quarterly* 2 (1) 12-14, 1971

2. The Association of Project Managers, *Body of Knowledge* (version 3) March 1996

3. Wirth, I, *How generic and how industry-specific is the project management profession?* International Journal of Project Management 14 (1) 7-11, 1996

Chapter 4

1. Belbin, M, *Management Teams: Why they succeed or fail* Butterworth Heinemann, Oxford

Hawksmere information

Hawksmere – quality programmes and practical value

Hawksmere is one of the UK's leading training organisations, providing high quality programmes allied to practical value. Every year we present around 450 public seminars as well as working with clients on a comprehensive range of in-company tailored training.

Our objective for each delegate

Our aim at every course is to provide each participant with added expertise, techniques and ideas of practical use. Our speakers are practitioners who are pre-eminent in their own field: as a result, the information and advice on offer are both expert and tried and tested.

Hawksmere offers you a broad in-depth range, from skills to strategies

Our programmes cover a wide range from management development to law, finance, insurance, government contracts and project management. They span all levels, from introductory skills to sophisticated techniques and the implications of complex legislation.

A continuing search for improvement

Our policy is to continue to re-examine and develop our successful courses, constantly updating and improving them. We offer a mixed range of one and two day public programmes, combined with some longer residential courses.

Our aim is to continue to anticipate the shifting, often complex challenges facing everyone in both the professions and industry, and to provide programmes of high quality, focused on producing practical results.

For further information on all our public seminars, call our Sales Department on 0171-824 8257.

Hawksmere In-Company

Hawksmere trainers are all professionals with sound practical experience. Our approach is participative, with extensive use of case studies and group work. The emphasis is on working with clients to define objectives, develop content and deliver in the appropriate way. This gives our client total flexibility and control. In our experience, direct client involvement and support are prime contributors to the success of any programme.

As with our public seminars, participants in Hawksmere In-Company programmes will receive a customised course manual produced to our own high standard which will serve as useful reference documentation after the course.

What can we offer you?

We can provide training in all the areas covered by our public seminar programmes as well as in other topics which you may identify.

In sum we can offer you:

- Tailored company programmes producing real results.
- Expert speakers matched to your company profile.
- Flexibility of time and place.
- Maximum impact on productivity through training your staff at a pace to suit you.
- Your total control over course content.
- Advice on the training needs of individuals.